OUT OF THE
HOUSE OF BONDAGE

Sourcebooks in Negro History

OUT OF THE
HOUSE OF BONDAGE

BY

KELLY MILLER

NEW INTRODUCTION BY

G. FRANKLIN EDWARDS

SCHOCKEN BOOKS · NEW YORK

INTRODUCTION TO THE 1971 EDITION

The essays of Kelly Miller included in this volume must be understood in terms of the temperament and intellectual perspective of the author and against the background of the racial climate in which they were written. Brought together and published in book form in 1914, the essays first appeared in various magazines during several years prior thereto. In the main, they represent Miller's views and analyses of significant developments in Negro life in the United States and of race relations as a product of racial contact in wider areas of the world. Most of the essays are focused upon the experiences of the Negro in the half century between emancipation and the time of publication, a period which covered most of the lifespan of the author, who was born in the year the Emancipation Proclamation was issued.

At the time these essays were written, the racial climate did not provide a basis for optimism regarding the future course of race relations. The sanguine views of the early Reconstruction years that the Negro would enjoy full participation in the American system had been dissipated by subsequent events, particularly those occurring between 1877 and the end of the nineteenth century, a period one historian has characterized as the nadir in race relations.[1] Political disfranchisement of the Negro and *de jure* segregation of the races were achieved by various devices, including the adoption of new constitutions and amendments to existing ones, a process which continued in the several southern states until 1910. Lynchings and other violent acts perpetrated against Negroes, though somewhat reduced from their high point of the 1890's, remained substantially high in 1910. Although nine-tenths of the Negro population lived in the South, with a majority residing on southern farms as tenants and sharecroppers, a drift to the cities had begun. Commenting on a 1913 symposium[2] which evaluated the progress of the Negro after fifty years of freedom, E. Franklin Frazier noted that "None of the contributors to this symposium could foresee at the time that the drift of Negroes to cities would develop, as the result of a world war, into a mass migration to northern cities which would change the relation of the Negro to American society. . . ."[3] The status of the Negro as a second-class citizen had been crystallized and appeared set for years to follow.

Despite the absence of a sound basis for optimism during the first fifteen years of the present century, Negro leaders were actively engaged in ideological discussions and controversy regarding programmatic efforts for racial uplift and advancement. The most celebrated of these was the DuBois–Washington debate over whether industrial or liberal education should be emphasized. This oversimplified statement obscures much of the philosophical differences between the two ideologies, their suggested strategies for training Negroes, and their practical consequences for race relations. It is mentioned here only to indicate that there was a rational concern with the problems of racial advancement and racial solidarity on the part of Negro intellectuals, schoolmen, and community leaders.[4]

Kelly Miller was more than an observer of the great debate. According to August Meier, he played the role of the "pragmatic harmonizer."[5] Although by inclination and temperament Miller was disposed to favor liberal education, as several of the essays in this volume indicate, the role of "pragmatic harmonizer" is illustrated in his essay "Fifty Years of Negro Education," in which he observes that, "Industrial and higher education are complementary factors of the same product. They are both essential parts of the educational program, each in its proper place and proportion. . . . It is perfectly evident that no one school, nor any single type of schools, is adequate to the wide circle of racial needs." The foregoing expression doubtless contributes to the assessment that "Perhaps more than any other single person Miller can be described as one who typified the thinking of the intellectual and professional elite in the age of Washington."[6]

I

For almost the entire period of his adult life, Kelly Miller was a professional educator, serving both as teacher and administrator at Howard University. He belonged to an early generation of educated Negroes, having received the baccalaureate degree from Howard in 1886. As many others of his generation, his rise from lowly social origins was marked by disciplined habits and a strong motivation for achievement. He worked at the U.S. Pension Office while an undergraduate to earn his expenses and, following the completion of his undergraduate degree, continued to work for a year as a government employee while taking private tutorials in mathematics and astronomy. This was followed by two years of study in mathematics at the Johns Hopkins University in 1887-1889. After a year as a teacher in the public schools of the District of Columbia, Miller began his career at Howard as a teacher of mathematics and served variously as Professor of Mathematics, Professor of Sociology, Dean of the College, and Dean of the Junior College. He retired from the University in 1934 and died in Washington, D.C., five years later.[7]

In the context of his own professional concern and his commitment to education, it is little wonder that several of the essays in this volume are directly concerned with the role of education as a contributor to racial advance. There is an appreciative assess-

ment of the role of the early missionaries in providing schools and instruction for Negroes and of
the role of philanthropy in providing facilities in
rural areas where they were most needed. The re-
duction of illiteracy by the public schools and the
role of higher education in training a leadership
cadre of professionals to administer to the Negro
masses are duly noted. In essence, education provided a major path on which the Negro advanced
out of the house of bondage. But it was not only the
instrumental value of education in qualifying for
jobs and leadership roles with which the author was
concerned; humanistic values were of equal importance to him.

In the essay "Education for Manhood," Miller
notes that the two major functions of education are
"(1) to develop and perfect the human qualities of
the individual, as a personality, and (2) to render
him a willing and competent participant, as an instrumentality, in the federation of the world's
work." Initiative, enjoyment, character, and service
are objectives of education, but these can be achieved
only if the educational process leads men to develop
a reverence for themselves as conscious personalities. It is, he avers, a hundred times more difficult to
make bricklayers men than to make men bricklayers.
Given the oppression of slavery and its violation of
human dignity and potential, "The educated Negro
today represents the first generation grown to the
fullness of manhood under the influence and power

of education. . . . The hope of the race is focused in them.''

Those who read these essays doubtless will note Miller's own broad education as reflected in his facile style, studded with quotations and examples taken from literature and mathematics. The impression one gains from reading the essays is of an artist enjoying his work, although impelled by a strong impulse to point out what, in his judgment, an appropriate education would contribute to the development of Negroes as personalities, following two and a half centuries of defilement in slavery.

II

The preoccupation with race relations in the United States and in other parts of the world doubtless led to Miller's interest in sociology. As early as 1903 he began to teach courses in this subject, and his essays reflect the influence of sociological analysis. In ''Out of the House of Bondage'' he analyzes the development of the Negro in terms of his acquisition of western civilization. It was as a phase of the ''contact, attrition and adjustment of the various races of man,'' a subject elaborated in his remarkable essay ''The Ultimate Race Problem,'' that Miller viewed the case of the Negro as having a special and unique interest. There should be no surprise, he stated, that the American Negro ''shows such little regard for the welfare of his native Con-

tinent and for his parent stock. The complete severance of his ties with Africa dictated that he would
take on the language, religion and general culture of
the dominant group.''

In a manner reminiscent of Lord Bryce's assessment of the Negro's progress, Miller thought the
advancement of the race in fifty years of freedom
represented one of the marvels of history. The Negro
had met the physical test of adjustment to a new
environment and the rigors of slave labor by increasing his numbers. He had shown a remarkable capacity for learning and had developed a professional
class of considerable stature. In the Negro church
he had manifested a capacity for institution building. Initiative and discipline were demonstrated by
his increasing acquisition of property.

The remarkable advance of Negroes resulted in
Miller's concluding that in time they would take
their place as full partners in American life. This
position was reached not only by extrapolation of
the rate of Negro advance but by an assessment
of the illogic of the caste system that existed during
the time the essays were written. ''Although the
Negro enjoys theoretically all the rights and prerogatives of an American citizen, yet in public sentiment and in actual practice he is fixed to an inferior
social, civil, political and industrial status. But this
scheme of subordination can be only local and temporary.''

The above conclusion reflects Miller's faith in

prediction from observed historical processes. Unlike some other analysts who envisaged a subordinate status for the Negro over a much longer period, Miller's belief in an ethic of change tied to education and its potential for social mobility led to an espousal of a more optimistic future for Negroes in American society. Unlike Du Bois, for example, who regarded the Negro's high visibility—color and other physical traits—as a virtually impermeable barrier to his achievement of equality and respect, Miller did not give physical traits such comparable importance in his analysis. For him, the evolution of like patterns of behavior was more important than physical differences. This is in contrast to Du Bois' observation that even with similar patterns of social conduct, rationalizations based upon race would continue to make the Negro an outcast.

One should not conclude that Miller was not fully aware of the stubborn nature of race prejudice and discrimination as formidable forces which had to be overcome. They, however, were not unyielding and could be surmounted as larger numbers of Negroes gained access to opportunities for contacts with wider areas of western civilization. The inevitable result of such a development would be an increased similarity in the manners, morals, and achievements of the Negro and whites.

The apparent illogical argument that what was required for Negro advance was greater opportunity for contacts with aspects of civilization, in spite of the persistence of prejudice and discrimination which denied such opportunities, is resolved by Miller's interpretation that contradictions and inconsistencies in the social process are self-correcting. Nowhere is this better expressed than in his essay "The American Negro as a Political Factor." While recognizing the importance of suffrage as a right preservative of all other rights, he notes that the Negro has been disfranchised by systematic methods based upon political machinations. But, he writes, "In this country political, social and economic conditions gravitate toward equality" and "Democratic institutions can no more tolerate a double political status than two standards of ethics or discrepant units of weights and measures." It is in the context of the larger process of social change that the Negro will be exposed to wider patterns of American behavior and become a fuller participant in its cultural life.

The exclusion of Negroes from the political life of the nation was, in Miller's judgment, one limiting factor to further progress of the group. But it was this exclusion from politics, as well as white domination of the economic, educational, and social life of the nation, which provided an opportunity for the Negro church to become a distinctive institution. "The Church," Miller stated, "is not merely a religious institution, but embraces all of the complex functions of Negro life."

One finds in his essay "The Ministry" a percep-

tive and excellent analysis of the Negro church as
an institution providing opportunities for self-expression and education of the Negro masses, and an
analysis of the leadership roles of the Negro minister in business and education, as well as in spiritual
matters. The classification of the types of Negro
churches, based on their relationship to and de-
pendence upon white denominations, and the assigned reasons for the dominance of those having
ecclesiastical independence represent functional
analysis at its best. It was the transcendent need of
the Negro masses for self-expression and for self-
government which gave the church its distinctive
cast and guaranteed its independence and importance.[8]

It should not be concluded that Miller was uniformly dispassionate in his analysis of race problems and race relations. At times, his approach
borders on the polemical, but his basic scholarly
approach serves to check broader excursions into
which his race pride and race consciousness would
have led him. His propensity to stick to the facts,
even amid passionate concern, is clearly evident in
his open letters to those whom he regarded as race
bigots and dogmatists and whose writings he thought
did the cause of the Negro infinite harm. For example, his reply to Thomas Dixon's charge that the
Negro was incapable of assimilating the culture of
the white man and his open letter to John Temple
Graves, whose inflammatory writing on race he re-

garded as contributing to the Atlanta Riot of 1906, though bitter in tone, are characterized by a mobilization of facts and polite restraint.[9] It is worth noting that his reply to Graves was entitled ''An Appeal to Reason on the Race Problem.''

III

At the outset it was stated that the essays included in this volume should be read against the background of the period in which they were written and in terms of what is known of the author's intellectual orientation and perspective. It is evident that Miller was an informed student of the race problem who was familiar with the social-science literature of his times. He brought to this literature a power of synthesis. As an essayist, he was able to add a critical analysis which showed balance and insight. He was an intellectual whose major commitment was to scholarly pursuits and to the university with which he was identified. At no time did he assume a leadership role in any activist organization, although he pointed out the need for organized programs to advance the cause of the Negro.

For those who regard as naive his faith that racial amity would emerge with the development of opportunities for Negroes, a conclusion derived from his understanding of historical processes, it should be noted that objective conditions at the time these essays were written were quite different from those which were to develop during the next half century. The mass migrations of Negroes to cities of the North and South which began shortly after the essays were written and continued over the next several decades to result in the Negro population's becoming the most urbanized segment in the country, could not have been foreseen. Nor could one have predicted in 1914 the scale to which massive ghettos with their pathologies and conflicts would develop, first in northern cities and later in southern urban communities. This extreme physical isolation of Negroes, taken along with their growing awareness of the inconsistencies between the ideals of society and their position in it, gave the race problem a different profile than it had when these essays were written. It is the improvement of the educational status of the masses, achieved by both formal and informal means, which has made the Negro population more acutely conscious of the differences between society's ideals of equality and their subordinate position. Appeals to unrest and race consciousness generated by these inconsistencies in American life are now being made by a group of Negro leaders in almost every field. They include a growing cadre of professional politicians whose importance for racial advance Miller recognized.

It remains to be pointed out that studies of race prejudice and discrimination and of the operations of the social system, particularly those made in the last quarter of a century, have improved our knowledge of race relations. The acceptance of racial minorities by majorities is not so easily achieved as a result of convergences in behavior patterns resulting from wider contacts. The inconsistencies between ideals and practices within a social system are not necessarily self-correcting. The role of legislation and expressions of power are more influential today in setting normative patterns in race relations than are reason, conscience, and tendencies inherent in social evolution, factors to which Miller attached such great importance.

These observations are not meant to detract from the value of the essays included in this volume. On the contrary, each has merit for the contribution it makes to our perspective on the race problem and race relations during the first decade of the present century. Collectively, they add to our understanding of the course over which race relations in this country developed, and they furnish us with insights into the intellectual qualifications and style of one of the most astute analysts of the early twentieth century.

G. FRANKLIN EDWARDS

Howard University
Washington, D.C.
July 1971

1. Rayford Logan, *The Negro in American Life and Thought, 1877-1901* (New York: Dial Press, 1954).

2. *The Negro Progress in Fifty Years* (Philadelphia: The American Academy of Political and Social Science, 1913).

3. E. Franklin Frazier, *The Negro in the United States,* rev. ed. (New York: The Macmillan Company, 1957), pp. 167-168.

4. For a full discussion of this controversy, see August Meier, *Negro Thought in America, 1880-1915* (Ann Arbor: University of Michigan Press, 1963), Part V, pp. 161 ff.

5. *Ibid.,* p. 217.

6. August Meier, *op. cit.,* p. 218.

7. These biographical materials are taken from the *Dictionary of American Biography,* Supplement 2, pp. 456-457; and Walter Dyson, *Howard University, The Capstone of Negro Eudcation: A History, 1867-1940* (The Graduate School, Howard University, 1941), p. 371.

8. Miller's analysis bears a close parallel to Frazier's. See E. Franklin Frazier, "The Negro Church: Nation Within a Nation," in *The Negro Church in America* (New York: Schocken Books, 1964), pp. 29-46.

9. The reply to Dixon, entitled "As to the Leopard's Spots" (1905), and his letter to Graves, "An Appeal to Reason on the Race Problem" (1906), were published in Miller's volume *Race Adjustment* (1908); the volume has been reprinted under the title *Radicals and Conservatives; and Other Essays on the Negro in America* (New York: Schocken Books, 1968).

PREFACE

The essays herein collected have appeared during the past few years in such magazines as *The Independent, The Atlantic Monthly, The Dial, The Nineteenth Century and After, The Educational Review, The Annals of the Academy of Political and Social Science, The Popular Science Monthly,* and *Neale's Monthly.* Acknowledgment and thanks are hereby rendered the above named publications for permission to use these papers in the present form. The titular essay appeared in *Neale's Monthly* for October, 1913.

While these essays do not pretend to offer a formal solution of the Race problem, yet it is believed that they deal with fundamental principles, and with issues that must be involved in any proposed scheme of solution.

K. M.

Howard University, Washington, D. C.

TABLE OF CONTENTS

OATH OF AFRO-AMERICAN YOUTH

I will never bring disgrace upon my race by any unworthy deed or dishonorable act. I will live a clean, decent, manly life; and will ever respect and defend the virtue and honor of womanhood; I will uphold and obey the just laws of my country and of the community in which I live, and will encourage others to do likewise; I will not allow prejudice, injustice, insult or outrage to cower my spirit or sour my soul; but will ever preserve the inner freedom of heart and conscience; I will not allow myself to be overcome of evil; but will strive to overcome evil with good; I will endeavor to develop and exert the best powers within me for my own personal improvement, and will strive unceasingly to quicken the sense of racial duty and responsibility; I will in all these ways aim to uplift my race so that, to everyone bound to it by ties of blood, it shall become a bond of ennoblement and not a byword of reproach.

A MORAL AXIOM

Which constitutes the Foreword as well as
the Final Word of this volume.

I hate a cat. The very sight
    Of the feline form evokes my wrath;
    Whene'er one goes across my path,
I shiver with instinctive fright.

And yet there is one little kit
    I treat with tender kindliness,
    The fondled pet of my darling, Bess;
For I love her and she loves it.

In earth beneath, as Heaven above,
    It satisfies the reasoning,
    That those who love the self-same thing
Must also one another love.

Then if our Father loveth all
    Mankind, of every clime and hue,
    Who loveth Him must love them, too;
It cannot otherwise befall.

OUT OF THE HOUSE OF BONDAGE

The story of the African on the American continent possesses both the painful reality of truth and the pleasing fascination of fiction. Although this story has been so frequently repeated as to become a wearisome recital, yet no sooner does the flagging public mind tire of the rehearsal than some accentuating feature demands it anew. This narrative will ever be fresh with perennial interest, not only because of the ever recurring dramatic incidents and episodes, but because its motif touches the hidden springs of the deepest human solicitude and passion. The continued performance of this never ending drama has already stretched through well-nigh three centuries, with not a hint of termination. The Emancipation Problem may be regarded as the close of the first act. The Golden Jubilee of this event justifies a moment's pause for a cursory glance at the past, a glimpse of the present, and, if it might be vouchsafed, an inkling of the future.

Three centuries ago two streams of population began to flow to the newer from the older continents of the world. The European component was but the natural overflow of the fountain of civilization, while the African confluent was forced upward from the lowest level of savagery. The confluence of these two streams has constituted our present population of some hundred million souls, divided into the approximate ratio of ten to one. Here we have the most gigantic instance in history of the hemispheric transference of population. The closest intimacy of contact of markedly dissimilar races gives the world its acutest and most interesting object lesson in race relationship. We are easily convinced that the whole movement must have been under the direction of a guiding hand higher than human intelligence or foresight. The deep cried unto the deep, and the nations heard and heeded the cry, although they little understood its far reaching meaning and import. The negro was introduced into this land by the European lord of creation, not as a fellow creature, but as a thing apart, destined to a lower range and scope by eternal and unalterable decree. This *tertium quid* was deemed a little more than animal and a little less than human. He was endowed with certain animal and mechanical powers which might justly be utilized and exploited for the glorification of the self-centred over-lord, to whom had been ordained dominion and power and glory forever. The exploitation of one race or individual for the aggrandization of another was the universally received and accepted doctrine of the age. Immediate economic advantage was the controlling motive. Greed for gain and glory takes little counsel of ultimate philosophy. Even so eminent an authority as Sir Harry Johnston tells us that ''there is sufficient of the devil still left in the white man for the 300 years' cruelties of negro (or other) slavery to be repeated, if it were worth the white man's while.'' Although the devil may still be dominant in the white man's breast, and it might seem, for the time being, profitable to reënact the iniquitous industrial régime of the past, yet the present state of knowledge of the far reaching consequences of economic and social laws would effectually forbid. Had there been three hundred years ago the faintest conception that this new-caught child of the tropics was endowed with human powers and aspirations that must ere long demand full satisfaction and acknowledgment, and had the enslavers been vouchsafed a glimpse of the tangled web of intricate issues involved in his enslavement, the tale

of two continents would now be different to
relate. The incident evils that have grown out
of the historic contact of these two races is
but the logical outcome of a shortsighted and
fatuous philosophy. The concomitant benefit
to human civilization now flowing, and destined
to flow from this contact, illustrates the sure
teaching of history, that an over-ruling Provi-
dence makes the wrath of man to praise him,
while holding the remainder of wrath in restraint.

All rational discussion must have a point of
departure. Before we can make any just ap-
praisement of the negro's progress during the
past fifty years we must project his achievements against the background of his inherent
or acquired capacities and equipment at the beginning of this period. Actual attainment
must be evaluated in terms of coincident helps
and hindrances. The significance of the crop
must be adjudged in light of the quality and
culture of the soil. It is wholly needless for
our purpose to discuss the native endowment
of the native African at the time of his trans-
plantation in America. It is finally sufficient
to describe his undisputed attainments gained
in the household of bondage, and his marvelous
development since his release.

Slavery was an institution of learning as

well as labor. The negro's taskmaster was also his schoolmaster. In order that he might accomplish the crude tasks imposed upon him, it was necessary that he should be instructed in the rudimentary principles and crude methods of its accomplishment. Efficiency as a tool depended upon his aptness as a pupil. Had the negro been inapt in understanding and inept in performance, he would have been unprofitable and, therefore, undesirable as a servant. The red Indian was not satisfactorily reduced to a condition of slavery, not merely because of the pugnaciousness of his spirit but also by reason of the stolidity of his understanding. He seemed to be hopelessly incapable of comprehending the white man's ways of doing things and the reason therefor. He lacked the negro's aptitude of mind and docility of disposition.

Slavery was always under the paradoxical necessity of developing the slave as an instrument while suppressing him as a person. Without a certain degree of intelligence the slave became useless; with too much intelligence he became dangerous. The fundamental fallacy of the institution lay in the supposition that one race or individual was predetermined for servile relationship to another. The biologists tell us that there is not found within the sphere of created things a single species with purposely altruistic function. Each species and individual is endowed with powers and prowess calculated to promote advancement after its kind. The predestined end and way of every creature is to advance its own well-being, the welfare of others being subserved incidentally and indirectly, if at all. Efficiency is not an altruistic virtue. The individual exerts his best powers only when he can visualize the efforts of his toil translated into terms of his own personal or tribal weal. To exploit human endeavor on any other hypothesis is to sin against the eternal cause. With a secret suspicion of this far sweeping truth, the master felt forced to limit the black man's activity to the crudest tasks, not because he was incapable of performing any other, but rather because he must not be initiated into the ulterior meaning and aim of the gospel of work. He must be kept in ignorance of the hidden meaning of things, lest he become restive under restraint and assert his human prerogative. There was a tinge of that primeval apprehension for fear the under man might stretch forth his hand and partake of the tree of knowledge and become as one of us. Nevertheless the negro became domesticated, if not educated, in the University of slavery, whose diploma admitted him to practice in the wide arena of the world's work. The narrator of the story of the negro is prone to touch too lightly upon the tutelage of servitude as being among the regrettable delenda of his experience in the household of bondage. But this discipline and experience formed his initiation into the civilizaton of the new world. All subsequent progress is based upon the foundation here laid.

Under the tuition of slavery the negro gained acquaintance with the English language, which is the most effective agency of civilization now operating on the face of the earth. All of the secrets of knowledge and culture are hidden in written and oral speech. There is nothing hidden that shall not be revealed to people who form acquaintance with the English tongue. The European child devotes the greater part of his time and effort to the acquisition of language because this is the key that unlocks the storehouse of the accumulated culture of the race. This is the gateway through which individuals and races must enter into the inheritance of the ages. The forms of language communicated to the negro under slavery were of the crudest and most imperfect character. The ear alone was initiated while the eye remained illiterate. Oral symbols of ideas might be imparted to the ear, but must not be presented to the eye or reproduced by hand. The process was limited to the short circuit of ear and tongue but the longer and more involved circuit of eye and finger was forbidden. The slave must be ear-minded alone; the master alone must be eye-minded. The black man was permitted to hear and speak but not to read and write. Even within the permitted range there were sharp and severe limitations. Only the simplest possible ideas were communicated in the most rudimentary terms. The recipient was supposed to understand only so much as he was expected immediately to execute. Not only must the higher ideas and ideals be withholden but also their forms of verbal expression. The negro knew nothing of the syntactical arrangement of the parts of speech nor the rules governing their meaning and use. The noun and the verb did not usually find themselves in agreement, nor was there any discoverable plan of grammatical law and order. Nevertheless he gained the essential function and power of the English language as a vehicle through which ideas are received and conveyed.

It was through slavery also that the negro was brought in touch with the Christian religion. The whole race, as if by magic, embraced this spiritual cult which appeals so powerfully to its own inner longings. Christianity affects the negro's spiritual nature as the sunlight writes its impression on the sensitized plate in photography. While the institution of slavery does not deserve the credit, it nevertheless afforded the occasion for the evangelization of the race. There was no adequate agency for this gigantic achievement. It doubtless would have taken centuries under ordinary missionary auspices to accomplish so great a result. The whole race, following the infallible logic of feeling, on first suggestion, embraced the new gospel which appealed at once to its inner disposition and outward situation.

The institution of slavery, as such, was necessarily averse to the evangelization of a subject race; for the mission of Christianity is to quicken the sense of inherent divinity easily translated into the more concrete terms of manhood. The desideratum of slavery was to inculcate a satisfied and complaisant servitude. The evangelization of the negro was accomplished through the stealthy process, so aptly described in that soul melting melody: "Steal away to Jesus." The humble slave with overtaxed body and overburdened soul, after the onerous task of the day's work, literally stole away to the low grounds and desolate places, in the loneliness of the midnight hour, and poured out his soul in anguish, where master might not molest, and none but God was near. Let the proud and haughty religionists, worshiping in marble temple, sitting before gilded altars in polished pews, and performing formal genuflections on cushioned knee-rests, disdain, if they will, these wild, incoherent spiritual longings of these despised and rejected creatures; but the sure satisfaction of their yearnings is the highest proof that our age affords that God still hears and answers prayer.

It is not necessary to say that the negro's religion was imperfect. People of imperfect development cannot have perfect accomplishments in any department of human excellence. Christianity found the negro in his humble and lowly estate, and appealed to his nature, just as he was, without one plea. Ignorance did not instantaneously give way to knowledge, corruption did not at once put on incorruption, nor did grossness immediately clothe itself with decorum and dignity of life. Unless the heavenly treasure were placed in earthen vessels, Christianity would find no lodgment among the frail children of men. If the test of perfection were to be applied, there would not be found a single Christian nation or race on the face of the earth, and indeed but few individuals. But the embracement of religion has been the chief factor in the progress of the negro race on this continent, and represents the highest gain that has come to it out of three centuries of contact with the Western world. This is the strongest tie that binds the negro in the ennobling bond of spiritual kinship to the fellowship of humanity.

The highest evidence of the essential quality of the negro's racial nature appears in his folk songs. Nowhere else does one find such perfect embodiment of the Christian graces of meekness, humility and forgiveness of spirit. Although subject to crushing conditions that would have caused any other race to vent its spirit in malediction, yet this race uttered the burden of its soul in these songs of sorrow, without the slightest tinge of bitterness, animosity or revenge. Such underlying soul-stuff is surely material meet for the kingdom of heaven.

Another inimitable quality which slavery developed out of the negro nature was manifested in the "black mammy." We search in vain the records of the human race for like indication of altruistic endowment and wealth of maternal affection. This crude, uncouth negro woman could take the child of her mistress

on one knee and her own offspring on another
and satisfy both out of the storehouse of her
mother love. By sheer force of this endowment, she was able to take the child of her cultivated mistress and foster for herself an attachment and endearment beyond that it bore
its own mother after the flesh. The undevi-
ating devotion of man-servant to master grew
out of the same spirit. Such instances of vicariousness on part of the race indicate the underlying soul quality of which they were but
fragmentary croppings. It is sometimes asserted that these qualities have not been transmitted to the new issue which seems prone to
display the opposite extreme of bumptious con-
ceitedness. The first effect of release from any
condition is apt to lead to its opposite. When
the pendulum is freed from one extreme of its
amplitude, it moves swiftly to the opposite
limit of its range. These are, however, but
fluctuating conditions due to shifting circumstances. Benevolence is essentially an altruistic virtue. Self-sacrifice is an inalienable co-
efficient of negro blood. The specific devotion
of maid-servant and man-servant under the
former régime is not destroyed by the overthrow of that régime, but is perpetuated and
carried forward to be manifested, it may be, in
other forms of outgiving. The South does well

to build a monument to the black mammy whose altruistic devotion is worthy to be perpetuated through all time. But let it never be forgotten that this memorial is not to her disinterested and detached devotion alone, but will stand as a perpetual reminder of the vicarious virtues of a sacrificial race.

The negroes were brought to America as disjected and expatriated individuals. The imported slaves represented the conquered and subdued, the despised and outcast of their own country and race. Taken from widely separated sections of the African continent, representing tribes divided by dialect, custom and feudal strife, there was naturally enough no common bond of union among the scattered fragments that were thrown together in a new and strange land. They were held together only by the outward compulsion of a common bondage and the facial compulsion of a common color. There was neither a common spirit, purpose nor impulse. Surprise is sometimes expressed that the American negro shows such little regard for the welfare of his native continent and for his parent racial stock. He was literally cut out off from the land of the living with a complete severance of ties. No ennobling or endearing stream of influence followed him across the sea. He was sustained by no comforting recollections of his native land. Had the first penal colonists of Georgia been permanently severed from the ennobling influence of their native England, and abandoned to the brooding recollection of their hard prison lot in the land from which they had escaped, we should hardly expect them to cultivate much reverential regard for the country or the people of their origin.

The negro had to develop as best he might a race consciousness, although it was the prudent policy and fixed purpose of the institution of slavery to frustrate its orderly and effective formation. Forbidden freedom of motion, means of intercommunication and the privilege of unconstrained assemblage, there was nevertheless the emergence of a crude race consciousness which was necessarily too feeble for effective service in the making of a race.

It should be added also that slavery contributed to the negro race a considerable infusion of white blood with whatever modifying or transforming power may be ascribed to the prepotency of that blood which is now dominant throughout the world. The American negro at the time of his emancipation, therefore, did not represent the African pure and simple, but the African plus a modifying modicum of European infusion and reinforcement.

The negro proved to be an apt pupil in taking on the general culture, manners and methods of his master. He quickly fell into his bias of mind and habits of thought, so much so that the psychic kinship of the negro and the Aryan seems much closer than that of breeds of nearer blood relationship. Imitation is the essential process by which culture is transmitted from age to age and from race to race. The imitator shows an appreciation of and a predilection toward the imitated attainment. Thus the negro, snatched from the wilds of savagery and plunged into the midst of a mighty civilization, received his preliminary preparation for his physical emancipation destined to come in the fullness of time.

The Emancipation Proclamation, demanded by the exigencies of war, destroyed, at one stroke, the institution of slavery which had been a thorn in the flesh of the nation from the time of its foundation. The remission of sin was not accomplished without the shedding of blood. This document is universally regarded as the world's greatest charter of liberty. A wave of altruistic ardor swept over the nation. The anti-slavery crusade showed as high a test of the Christ's spirit as has been afforded in all the list of Christian years. When the great deed had been done the whole nation burst forth in one triumphant song of moral elation, "Mine eyes have seen the glory of the coming of the Lord." Statesmanship and philanthropy vied with each other in their ministration to the new made freed-man. He was clothed with the full prerogative of citizenship and placed in competition with the strongest and most aggressive people on the face of the earth. The experience was indeed a stupendous one. But the African was not left alone in his upward struggle. A generous philanthropy furnished him schools and colleges in which the choice youth of his blood might partake of the secret and method of civilization and show them unto their more benighted brethren. A wise and discerning statemanship furnished schools for the education of the young. He was invited to partake of the tree of knowledge which he had neither planted nor watered. The current of public sentiment ran high in his favor. It was worth the price of public favor for anyone in high place to say harsh or unkind words against the least of these. Privilege and prerogative were accorded him which others had purchased at great price. No other submerged race ever enjoyed so profuse a measure of public favor as did the negro for a season. He proved to be an apt pupil and showed surprising acquisitive and inquisitive power. It seemed for a time that he would be the perpetual recipient of this favor. But the tide of public sentiment ebbs and flows like the waves of the sea. The black man has been both the beneficiary and victim of its sportive caprice. If to-day the current against him seems to be running cold and chilly, to-morrow it may be tempered again with the general warmth of human kindliness and sympathy. Any hopelessly submerged people entrapped in an environment such as his must depend largely upon the force of public sentiment.

The upward progress of the negro since his emancipation has not been a smooth and unhindered path. Indeed, the pathway of progress has never been a straight line, but always a zigzag course between the forces of right and wrong, justice and injustice, goodness and evil, cruelty and mercy. The journey from Egyptian bondage to the promised land beyond the Jordan could not be made by steam and electricity, but must be accomplished by the slowly moving caravan amidst the dangers and vicissitudes of the desert. While the negro has manifested the virtues of his status he has also shown the imperfection of his lot. His follies and frailties have been such as usually attach themselves to his class and condition. He is neither angelic nor diabolic, but simply human, with vice and virtues, excellences and imperfections such as befall the lot of man laboring under such burdens.

The advancement of the race during the past fifty years has been the marvel of the world. By universal agreement it is conceded that no people in the similar interval of time has made such wonderful strides in the ways of civilization. This progress is as unique as the contrasted helps and hindrances amidst which it has been attained have been striking. Progress cannot be finally evaluated in the terms of material units. Such standards do not constitute the best gauge of advancement toward the goal of human striving. The essential thing is to determine how far the postulant people have acquired the capacity, the equipment, appreciation and the purpose to become not merely recipients but partakers of the life and spirit and power of that civilization of which they would constitute a part. Material substances and outward forms of progress are but manifestations of the inner attitude and spirit.

Fifty years is entirely too short a time to measure the potency and promise of the race. In the economy of racial life a half century is scarcely more than a single year in the experience of an individual. It is the preparation period for rooting and grounding itself in the fundamental understanding and appreciation of the underlying principle of things. The things already accomplished or achieved should be regarded as but the first fruit and the earnest of larger things to come.

Rather than describe the progress of the race in terms of definite data and tabular array of ascertained facts after the manner of the statistician, let us, if we may, clothe the dry bones of bare facts with the vital power of the living truth.

Physical persistence is the fundamental test of civilization. If the red Indian does not live he cannot become civilized. On the other hand, if the negro continues to live and multiply he cannot escape the happy lot. It is small wonder that the social philosophers of a generation ago prophesied that the negro would speedily disappear under the stress of Aryan competition and arrogance, for what other weaker race can stand and withstand contact and attrition of the dauntless Teuton, and live? After the lapse of a half century of freedom, four and one half million slaves have doubled their number, under the strain and stress of conditions that would have caused almost any other of the weaker breeds of men to pine away and die. Eliminating foreign reinforce-

ment, the negro outstrides the European element of our population in the natural rate of
increase. The presence and promise of the negro race in the Western world is a clear ful-
fillment of that beatitude of promise, "Blessed
are the meek for they shall inherit the earth."
There are twenty-five millions of negroes on
the Western hemisphere, who through physical
persistence and a spirit of meekness have multiplied and thriven and are destined to inherit
all of the accumulated and transmitted civilization and culture of the ages. It requires no
gift of prophecy to predict that the American
negro will enter into this inheritance as heir
and joint-heir in the patrimony of mankind.

The discipline of slavery, though valuable as
a preliminary training, was, nevertheless, subject to such severe limitations that it illy fitted
the recipient for the competitive life of the
freeman. In the very nature of the case it
would impart only the passive and inert virtues. It made no appeal to the spirit of thrift,
economy, independence, enterprise and initiative. These virtues, essential in the freeman,
were discouraged in the slave. The method of
slavery was that of domestication as distin-
guished from the process of education, as that
term is nowadays wont to be interpreted.
Through domestication certain fundamental

and easily communicable qualities were transmitted by familiarity, association and contact
with the surcharged environment. This process necessarily preceded the formal method of
pedagogy in the experience of both the individual and the race. Under slavery the negro was
given the process without the principle, the
knack without the knowledge. The essential
basis of education is that it leads the recipient
to an understanding of the underlying principle, use and function of things. The slave was
told the relative distance between two rows of
cotton or hills of corn as a working formula,
but knew nothing of the laws controlling the
growth and culture of plants, nor the rules of
the market governing their distribution. Indeed he was not supposed to understand the
ultimate meaning and purpose of a single feature of life, but was directed to do things for
the ulterior benefit of the director. Education
had to begin where domestication left off. The
effort of the past fifty years on the part of this
race has been largely devoted to education in
the sense of understanding and making definite
the meaning and purpose of the formulas acquired under slavery. The rapidity with which
this race has become literalized is considered
its most marvelous attainment during the past
half century. In a period of fifty years a con-

siderable majority of its numbers have learned
the use of letters. This is a much larger per
cent. than is shown by many of the historic
races of the older world. The mere technical
acquisition of the use of letters is from one
standpoint a very simple attainment. A few
months' schooling is sufficient to communicate
to the individual the symbols of knowledge and
the method of combining them into written and
spoken speech. But, unless this attainment is
built upon a previous conception of the meaning and aim of the accumulated body of knowledge to which it leads, it is a comparatively
useless attainment. The key to the storehouse
of accumulated wisdom and experience of mankind is useless unless the wielder has a previous appreciation for the values which that
storehouse contains. The red Indian might
acquire the ability to read and write within
a single generation, but if he still clings to his
ancestral ways, and without the curiosity to understand the secret and method of civilization
or the desire to avail himself of them, his technical acquisition would be little more than a
curious intellectual gymnastic. But the negro
had already had a foretaste of the white man's
civilization vouchsafed through the institution
of slavery. This simply whetted his appetite
for the fuller understanding of the things

which had been withholden. Just as the child
does not gain from the school his first conception of the meaning and use of things, but
merely learns to correlate ear and tongue, eye
and finger in speech facility and general understanding, so the negro, who has already received his initial tuition through slavery,
grasped eagerly the opportunity to strengthen
and enlarge his acquisition through the process
of literalization. His schooling so far has
mainly strengthened and confirmed what had
already been acquired by contact and use, and
laid the basis for still greater accomplishment. The first effect of knowledge is potential
rather than practical. The application to actual
life conditions comes only after the knowledge
is absorbed and assimilated. So far, the energy of the race has been absorbed in the process of acquisition. The period of application
has just begun. It is noticeable that any element of the white population makes a much
greater use of a given amount of knowledge
than does the negro at the present time. The
ways of knowledge are comparatively new to
him, and a larger part of his energy is con-
sumed in grasping its meaning and, therefore,
the dynamic residue is correspondingly dim-
inished. On the other hand, the white race already possesses the meaning and spirit and

power of civilization, even though the individual man be illiterate. Within the next fifty years we may expect to see the negro apply his knowledge to things concrete to a degree not yet dreamed of. This is more than a question of industrial or technical training, but involves the larger issue of applying thought to things. The thought must precede the application. The Anglo-Saxon race never needs any particular kind of education to accomplish any desired task. It comprehends the nature and purpose of the task and quickly devises means of its accomplishment. "To do with your might what your hands find to do" is a mistaken and inverted motto. The proper form should run, "To do with your hands what your mind finds to do." The material accumulation of the negro, marvelous as it seems, is but an incident of his general education. The great value of the knowledge which he has received is that it has indoctrinated him into the ideas and spirit of the world around him. This indoctrination cannot but shortly bear adequate fruit in terms of concrete attainment.

Whenever a single individual of the race becomes literate, he has gained an everlasting acquisition which in all probability will be handed down from generation to generation, and become more effective with each transmission. It is hardly conceivable that literate parents will ever rear illiterate offspring. A race with the curiosity and ambition of the negro, which has once gained possession of the golden key of knowledge with its twenty-six notches unlocking all of the secrets of things, can hardly be held back from full realization of all that there is in store.

The accumulation of houses and lands and material goods on the part of the negro has been commendable and encouraging. If his landed possessions could be formed into one continuous area, it would make a territory larger than many a far famed principality in ancient and modern annals.

In industry he has pushed his way into every line of listed occupation and contributes his full share to the nation's industrial equation.

He has developed a professional class who sprang into existence suddenly like Melchisedeck of old, without antecedent or beginning of days. This professional class must stand in the high places of leadership and guidance of the masses and direct them aright amid the stress and strain of a strenuous civilization. It is easy to predict the speedy undoing of a race that fails to produce its own competent leaders. A people that can produce safe and sagacious leadership can never be undone.

In religion, the race has developed a priesthood whose increasing power and piety will enable them to hold this vast Christian constituency in definite organic relation to the great religious movements of the age.

In morals, manners, social customs and habits he conforms to the prevailing standards, with no greater variation than grows out of his status in the general scheme. The negro shows his near kinship to the great body of white Americans by speaking the same language, worshiping the same God, striving after the same ideals, longing for the same destiny. None but the most confirmed pessimist can say that that past half century has not given a satisfactory indication that he will be able to meet every exaction that the coming years may impose upon him.

The case of the negro in America, though of striking and unique interest, is but a part of the great problem of contact, attrition and adjustment of the various races of man which has filled the pages of history, is now operating in all the ends of the earth, and is projected to the ages yet to be.

· The function of the prophet is to tell us of the future. He peeps over the horizon of the present and gives his fellowmen, of duller vision, a hint of coming events. He does not see any particular isolated future occurrence, but his deeper insight enables him to forecast the drift and tendency of things. The true poet is gifted with clairvoyant power. He visualizes future events with unerring certainty. The prophet Isaiah deserves the highest rank in this class. The messianic appropriation of his prophecy has robbed it of the universality of its application. All true prophecies apply to universal human conditions, and the unfolding of human experience will furnish their perpetual fulfilment. The prophet embodies the feeling and aspiration of those who suffer and gives prophetic utterance of their hope of relief. He voices the eternal utterings of the man farthest down, who will ever find in the circumstances of his lot perennial fulfilment of prophecy. The Hebrew prophet's utterances apply with all but absolute accuracy, even in detail and minutia, to the relative circumstances and situation of the white race and the negro of the American soil. Not a line, scarcely a word, can be omitted from the description without seriously impairing the analogy.

Isaiah, 53rd Chapter:

For he shall grow up before him as a tender plant, and as a root out of dry ground; he hath no form nor comeliness; and when we shall see him, there is no beauty that we should desire him.

He is despised and rejected of men; a man of sorrow and acquainted with grief; and we hid as it were our faces from him; he was despised, and we esteemed him not.

Surely he hath borne our grief, and carried our sorrow: yet we did not esteem him stricken, smitten of God and afflicted.

But he was wounded for our transgressions, he was bruised for our iniquities; the chastisement of our peace was upon him; and with his stripes we are healed.

All we, like sheep, have gone astray; we have turned every one to his own way; and the Lord hath laid on him the iniquity of us all.

He was oppressed, and he was afflicted, yet he opened not his mouth; he is brought as a lamb to the slaughter, and as a sheep before her shearers is dumb, so he openeth not his mouth.

He was taken from prison and from judgment; and who shall declare his generation? for he was cut off out of the land of the living: for the transgressions of my people was he stricken.

And he made his grave with the wicked, and with the rich in his death, because he had done no violence, neither was any deceit in his mouth.

Yet it pleased the Lord to bruise him; he hath put him to grief: when thou shalt make his soul an offering for sin, he shall see his seed, he shall prolong his days, and the pleasure of the Lord shall prosper in his hand.

He shall see of the travail of his soul, and shall be satisfied: by his knowledge shall my righteous servant justify many; for he shall bear their iniquities.

Therefore will I divide him a portion with the great,

and he shall divide the spoil with the strong; because he hath poured out his soul unto death: and he was numbered with the transgressors; and he bore the sin of many, and made intercession for the transgressors.

The hardships and tribulation and vicarious function of this prophecy have already been fulfilled on the part of the negro by three centuries of toil and anguish; the triumph and glorification of it are now fulfilling and seem clearly destined to be wholly fulfilled. When the white race awakens to a quickening sense of the sacrificial function of this transplanted race; how it has done the rough work of the nation; how it has relieved their own sons and daughters from the lower range of toil and released them for thee.

THE PHYSICAL DESTINY OF THE AMERICAN NEGRO

America has been called the universal melting pot, in which the various nationalities of Europe are to be fused into one homogeneous type. This alembic, however, is supposed to affect only the different branches of the Aryan race. The accepted assimilative process is not universal in its scope, but is limited to the continent of Europe. The white races alone are deemed eligible components of the desired compound. The polychrome races and sub-races of Asia, Africa, and the scattered islands of the seas are not considered as contributory factors to the forthcoming composite American type.

The primal passion of mankind recognizes no ethnic limitations or physical barriers of race, but results in fusion of blood wherever it has unconstrained exercise and scope. Racial antipathies real or alleged, political pronouncements, religious inhibition, social proscription, all break down in face of the cosmic

urge to multiply and replenish the earth. The
sons of God, in their supercilious security,
never fail to look lustfully upon the daughters
of men, while shielding their own sisters from
the embraces of the lower order of males. The
composite progeny is the offspring of the male
sex of the stronger race and the female sex
of the weaker; but, in the final fetching up of
things, the same results will be accomplished.
Wherever different racial elements are brought
into proximity, physical separation can be safeguarded only by legislative enactment, religious sanction, and the excitation of race antipathy by artificial stimulus. Universal experience shows that natural aversion of races does
not possess strength and stubbornness to preserve purity of breed.

The white race in America is put to its wit's
end to keep its racial stock free from the taint
of Asiatic and African blood. A monochrome
civilization presents the prevalent ideal. At
present it presents the spell and power of religious frenzy. Under the sanction of this
craze, it is considered more blessed to be white
than to be right. A polychrome social scheme
is deemed abominable to God and man. An
inspirited race consciousness is growing
keener and keener with the passing years.
This consciousness is based upon physical

rather than psychical likeness. The bond of brotherhood includes those who are born of the flesh rather than those who are born of the spirit. Superficial distinction of color counts for more than cult or creed.

Patriotic fervor or emotional zeal may beget emotional solidarity which entirely overleaps the cleavage of race or color. The triumph of Islam is a concrete, living embodiment of this principle. The ideal of Christianity is that all of its devotees, regardless of ethnic deviation, are baptized into one spirit, in which there is neither Jew nor Greek, Barbarian, Scythian, bond or free. The Christian creed is absolutely incompatible with the caste of color. Spiritual kinship transcends all other relations among men. The proclaimed purpose of this religion is to establish peace and good will on earth, but there is a wide margin between the proclaimed purpose and practical operation of this religion, especially as it relates itself to the Teutonic branch of the white race. Its chief beneficial effect is seen in the minor merciful ministrations of charity, but nowhere has it dominated the tough Teutonic spirit of race intolerance. The Protestant Christian in dealing with other races of men, passively acquiesces in the doctrine of the equality of the soul, but stubbornly balks at social equality. A continuance of this exclusive spirit on the part of the dominant race in America is as certain as any other calculable force concerning which we have predictive data. If the undesirable element be black, like the negro, it is excluded from the social scheme on the ground of inferiority. If it be yellow, like the Japanese, it meets with a like fate because of suspected superiority. So feeble is the force of logic against the dominating purpose of an arrogant race!

It must be taken for granted in the final outcome of things that the color line will be wholly obliterated. While blood may be thicker than water, it does not possess the spissitude or inherency of everlasting principle. The brotherhood of man is more fundamental than the fellowship of race. A physical and spiritual identity of all peoples occupying common territory is a logical necessity of thought. The clear seeing mind refuses to yield or give its assent to any other ultimate conclusion. This consummation, however, is far too removed from the sphere of present probability to have decisive influence upon practical procedure. It runs parallel with the prophecy that every valley shall be exalted and every hill shall be brought low. This is a physical necessity. Under the continuing law of gravitation, every stream that trickles down the mountain side, every downpour of rain, and every passing gust of wind removes infinite particles and shifts them from a higher to a lower level. This tendency to lower the one and lift the other will continue everlastingly until equality has been established as the final condition of stable equilibrium. In the meantime, however, the human race must adjust itself to the existence of mountain and valley as a lasting, if not everlasting, reality. Likewise, perpetual attrition of races must ultimately wear away all distinction and result in a universal blend. But the approximation of this goal is too slow and imperceptible to have any effect upon the present plan of race adjustment. We are concerned with persistent, stubborn realities which we have the power neither to influence nor affect, and must deal with conditions as they are in our day and generation, and not as we may vainly or vaguely imagine them in the ages yet to be. The time-server is often considered as a designation of reproach, but finite comprehension can only serve its day and generation. It requires omniscience to serve eternity.

The absence of the brown, the rapid extermination of the red, and the forced exclusion of the yellow leave the white and black races

as residuary constituents in the drama of race
adjustment on this continent. The rapid as-
similation of European nationalities into one
homogeneous type proceeds apace without
noise or notice. The negro element, too, is
slowly developing an ethnic solidarity which
indicates its immediate, if not ultimate, physical destiny in this land.

In current discussion the term ''negro'' is
used loosely to designate those people whose
maternal ancestors were imported as slaves
from the continent of Africa. While the term
ordinarily denotes color, it also connotes condition. The social segregation of the colored
race is based no less upon its traditional servile status than upon ethnic characteristics.

The American negro, as he is called, does
not constitute a race in the sense of a compact,
ethnic group, imbued with a common spirit and
impelled by a common impulse. There is no
solidified physical basis as a background for
the emergence of a common consciousness with
a strength and stubbornness to compel a co-
ordinate policy of persistent procedure. There
is rather a promiscuous assortment of individuals with diverse physical and spiritual dispo-
sitions and actuated by the antagonistic instinct
of the Ishmaelite. Psychologists tell us that
a collective soul emerges most easily from a

basis of physical likeness either through its inherent predisposition or by force of external compulsion. The imported slaves were disjected and expatriated individuals snatched from wide apart geographical areas, and captured from tribes differing widely in cult, custom and color.

The white race has never failed to infuse its blood into the veins of inferior races with whom it has come in contact. We are told in Greek mythology that Father Chronos devoured the offspring of his lust as soon as they were born, in order to avoid future complications of a troublesome issue. The Teutonic races seek to accomplish the same end by relegating their composite progeny to the lower status of the mother race. This policy is intended to preserve the purity of the stronger race while it mixes the blood of the weaker. The prepotent influence of the male progenitor upon the progeny is left out of account. The Latin races, on the other hand, incorporate the offspring of the dominant male and the dominated female, thus affecting a mixture of the white while preserving the purity of the darker breed. The immediate effect of the Teutonic policy may be agreeable, for the time being, to its Aryan arrogance, but there must, at some time, come a reckoning for the awful conse-

quences of visiting the lustful burden of one
race upon another.

The negro woman has been made to bear the
brunt of the evil passions of all the races of
men living or sojourning in this country.
Within the veins of the so-called negro race
there course traces of the blood of every known
variety or sub-variety of the human family.
Not only within the limits of the race itself,
but even within the veins of the same individuals, the strains of blood are mingled and
blended in inextricable confusion. Indeed, if
there be such a thing as natural race antipathy,
the negro, both as a race and as an individual, would be confronted by fightings within
and fires without. The task of fusing these
people into a common ethnic unity constitutes
its primary problem. The institution of slavery fostered a spirit of internal antagonism.
Every safeguard was taken to prevent the
emergence of an effective social consciousness.
Wherever two or three negroes were gathered
together, a white man was set in the midst of
them to frustrate any attempt at coördinate
purposes.

The Jewish race has preserved its physical
identity for two thousand years, albeit the
overflow of its blood has been transfused into

all nations among which the Jew has sojourned. The integrity of this race, however, has been preserved through spiritual sanction rather than by physical or racial proclivity.

It must be conceded that the quickest solution of the American race problem would be the immediate physical absorption of the negro element in the white race; but this is not possible, due to the universal attitude of the dominant race toward miscegenation.

The weaker race cannot force itself upon the stronger except through universal prostitution, a policy which is too repugnant to the moral sense to be contemplated as a racial policy. The American negro will be compelled to preserve his social and physical solidarity for many years to come through force of external compulsion. He is subject to conditions which he did not create and cannot control. The negro race in this country must become one with itself before it can become one with the American people.

The Federal Census shows unmistakably the drift of the negro population toward the formation of a new sub-race. This coming race will be composed of African-European blood, and its color will not be black, but a yellowish brown.

Negro and mulatto population of the U. S. from 1850
to 1910:

				Per Cent.
Year	Tot. Colored	Black	Mulatto	Mulatto
1850	3,638,808	3,233,057	405,751	11.2
1860	4,441,830	3,853,467	588,363	13.2
1870	4,880,009	4,295,960	583,049	12.0
1890	7,470,040	6,337,980	1,132,060	15.2
1910	9,828,294	7,766,894	2,051,400	20.9

Strictly speaking, the term mulatto includes
only the first offspring of white and black parents, but, in the census sense of the term, it
contemplates all persons who show some per-
ceptible trace of negro blood.   Due allowance
must also be made for discrepant definitions
of the terms at the several census decades.   The
well known inaccuracies of the census of 1870
are clearly disclosed in this table.   But, after
making all possible allowances, there is a persistent tendency toward a wider and wider distribution of the white blood already injected
into the negro race.   This tendency will inevitably continue until there has been an equable
diffusion throughout the entire mass.   During
the past twenty years the so-called mulatto
element increased 82 per cent., while the blacks
increased only 23 per cent.   The rapid relative
increase of the mixed element indicates clearly
the physical destiny of the race.   This increase

is maintained in every Southern state. In the Northern and Western states the black element has gained somewhat on the mulatto during the past twenty years. During the days of slavery many slaves were freed by their father-masters, or, as more frequently happened, were given opportunity to work out their freedom on easy terms, and were either sent or voluntarily migrated to the free states. The blacks rarely enjoyed such privileges. In 1850 there were more mulattoes than blacks in Maine, New Hampshire, Michigan, Wisconsin and Ohio. In every instance, however, the blacks predominated in the census of 1910. Since emancipation there has been a constant stream of emigration to the free states composed largely of blacks.

The rapid growth of the mulatto element is not due in any great degree to its inherent fecundity. The mulatto birth-rate is probably considerably lower and the death-rate higher than that of the blacks under similar conditions of living. This conclusion is forced by the fact that the mulattoes are found mainly in the Northern states and in the cities and towns where the birth-rate is lower and the death-rate higher than in the rural communities where the blacks predominate.

Every fresh infusion of white blood increases

the mulatto element at the expense of the black.
The black woman who has a number of children
by a white father would probably have borne
as many or more had she yoked with a black
spouse instead of a white paramour. The rise
and spread of the mixed element has not in
any degree increased the numerical strength
of the colored race. They have merely over-
lapped a like number of blacks. The lighter
color gains upon the darker, like the illuminant
upon the darkened surface of the waxing moon,
without increasing the total surface of the lunar orb. The mulatto offspring of a white parentage may be regarded as a continuing though
rapidly diminishing factor in the equation of
the negro population. There is not likely to
be much further direct infusion of white blood
into the negro race.

Under the institution of slavery the negro
was suppressed below the level of self-respect.
The black woman often felt her superior importance by becoming the mother of a tawny
child. The white master or overseer felt no
legal, social, or conscientious constraint in
victimizing the female chattel. Had this institution continued for another hundred years
without further importation of blacks from the
continent of Africa, the race would probably
have been well bleached through this libidinous

process. But the growing sense of self-respect and decency on the part of the black, as well as restraints of law and conscience on the part of the white man, has checked, if not halted, this outrageous procedure. The establishment of domestic ties and social standards in colored society effectively forbids such illicit relationship and makes outcasts of all such issue.

The laws of the Southern states forbidding intermarriage and social proximity of the races will absolutely prevent legitimate mulatto offspring. The social sensibilities of both races are at present so delicate on this issue that intermarriage would be exceedingly rare even if there were no forbidding laws. In the North, where there is no such restrictive law, the illegitimate offspring is so small as to be a negligible factor. The over-zealous quest of the negro prize-fighter for a white spouse so aroused the emotional frenzy of her race that it caused a half dozen state legislatures to contemplate enacting miscegenation laws.

Whatever illicit intercourse may still continue between the races at the present day, it is not likely to result in issue, as it was once wont to do. It partakes rather of the nature of the vice of the city slums and of the red light district, and it is an entirely different process from the old order of complaisant concubinage. The rise of the "sage femme" and the practice of race suicide tend to the same conclusion.

The segregation of the races, both in cities and in the rural districts, will lessen the opportunity for illicit offspring. In the large cities the negroes are segregated in wards and sections. In the Southern states, where they reside in greatest numbers, the black belts and sections are growing blacker and the white communities are growing whiter, indicating the metes and bounds of racial residence. This segregative tendency is wholly apart from and independent of the recent attempt to fix the bounds of the negro's habitation by law. In the sections where the negro resides the presence of the white man is not expected except in a purely business capacity. Illicit relationship will decrease in proportion to the separation of the areas of domicile.

As an illustration of the infrequency of the direct mulatto progeny, the student body of Howard University, about fifteen hundred in number, is composed largely of the mixed element. There are probably not a half dozen children of white parents in this entire number. On the other hand, the first pupils in this institution, a generation ago, were very largely the offspring of such parentage. The ones who are of lighest hue and show closest physical similarity to the white race are known to be the legitimate children of a colored co-parency. Of the more than two million so-called mulattoes in the colored race, an overwhelming number, especially of the younger generation, are offspring of colored fathers and mothers. It is safe to say that they average about one-fourth of the full measure of white blood. This would be equivalent to a half million full blooded white men who have become absorbed in the colored race. This European blood cannot remain in any one compartment of the race, but will tend to diffuse itself throughout the entire mass until it has assumed an approximate oneness in color and physical likeness. The process of diffusion will be facilitated by the well known tendency of the male to mate with the female of lighter hue. The poet Dunbar speaks of the swarthy maid with her swarthier swain as typical of this tendency.

In the census of 1890 some attempt was made to differentiate the mulatto element according to the degree of blood composition. The results showed that there were 105,136 quadroons, and 69,936 octoroons, and 967,988 mulattoes. The proportion of negro blood in the quadroon and octoroon elements represents over 30,000 full blooded negroes. Many of this

class have crossed or are likely to cross the
social divide and incorporate themselves into
the white race, in order to escape the nether
status of the despised blood. In some states a
person with only one-eighth negro blood in
his veins is given legal status with the white
race. These racial transmigrants carry with
them as much of negro blood as can easily be
concealed under an albicant skin and unkinked
hair. The white race will take only such homeo-
pathic dashes of negro blood as to remain substantially pure. It is reasonable to assume that
the equivalent of 50,000 full blooded blacks
have or are likely to be thus incorporated into
the white race. The transition of the quadroon
and octoroon classes will tend to widen the
physical margin between the two races.

There is unmistakable evidence that, in the
birth-rate of the mulatto element, the female
offspring is more numerous than the male.
The octoroon and quadroon male can more
easily conceal their negroid origin and clandestinely pass over to the white race than the
corresponding female. These factors leave a
considerable surplus of female mulattoes over
the corresponding male element. This gives
the darker male a wider area for his well
known propensity to mate with the lighter fe-

male, and will thus facilitate the rapid diffusion of this blood throughout the race.

A careful observation of negro schools, churches and miscellaneous gatherings in all parts of the country convinces the writer that fully three-fourths of the rising generation of the race have some traceable measure of white blood in their veins. The negro school, especially in the cities and towns, has about as many children of the unadulterated negro type as of the other extremes which cannot be easily detected from white. Both extremes, however, are a rapidly diminishing quantity, while the average of the race is approaching a medium of yellowish brown rather than black. We must take into account, also, the fact that a considerable portion of white blood can be wholly concealed under a negro exterior, which may reappear in the next generation. Within the next three or four generations the pure negro will be hard to find outside of the black belts and rural portions of the South and a new race will have arisen.

Science is of value to man only in proportion as it becomes predictive and enables him to adjust himself in harmony with foreseen events which he can neither alter nor control. The Weather Bureau at Washington forecasts the coming of frost and storm, so that the pru-

dent farmer may cover his crop and the sailor
seek shelter on the shore. A clear indication
of the physical destiny of the colored race
ought to enable us to deal more effectively
with the complicated features of this perplex-
ing problem and, at the same time, free the
white man from the frantic dread of amalgamation which now harasses his waking hours
and haunts him in his dreams.

EDUCATION FOR MANHOOD

The well known and well worn maxim of the poet, Lowell:

"New occasions teach new duties,
Time makes ancient good uncouth,"

expressed, with practical shrewdness, a transient phase, rather than the permanent form of truth. Good in the positive, or even in the comparative, degree may, indeed, be limited by circumstances, time and place; but superlative good is of the nature and essence of things eternal. A shallow philosophy emphasizes the evanescent phase of things rather than their permanent and enduring quality. To the superficial observer the world would seem to be one continuous panorama of evanescent issues. Practical wisdom would seem to be the only effective wisdom.

Opportuneness seems to be the controlling virtue. The man who is wise in his day and generation must catch the manners living as they rise, or they will forever elude his grasp.

The wisdom of one age becomes the folly of
the next. The schoolboy of to-day laughs at
the erudition of the ancient sage. The theories
which passed as marvels of knowledge a generation ago are now regarded as curious sur-
vivals of the intellectual dark ages. Celebrated works on science, philosophy and social
polity which once held the world under the dominion of their dogma are now relegated to
the moth and dust of oblivion. The path of
progress is strewn with the derelict of dis-
carded and discredited theories. The science
of yesterday, to-day, is science but falsely so-
called.

> "We call our fathers fools, so wise we grow,
>   Our wiser sons, no doubt, will call us so."

But a deeper philosophy gives a more comprehensive and far reaching vision. Essential
truth transcends the mutation of time and the
vicissitude of condition, and perdures from
everlasting to everlasting. The waves of the
sea may fluctuate with the shifting phases of
the moon; the lunar orb herself may wax and
wane in her periodic relations to earth, sun and
stars; but our solar system sweeps on forever
along its trackless path through space. According to the laws of grammar, everlasting
fact and unchangeable truth is not subject to

syntactical variations, but is always expressed
in the present tense and active voice. It is the
voice of truth issuing eternally from the burning bush: ''Before Abraham was, I am.'' The
educational philosopher must have a clear understanding of the relative place and importance of things incidental and things essential,
of things timely and things timeless, of things
transient and things eternal.

Education has two clearly differentiable
functions, (1) to develop and perfect the human qualities of the individual, as a personality, and (2) to render him a willing and competent participant, as an instrumentality, in the
federation of the world's work. The one in-
heres in the nature of man and is conditioned
only by the innate economy of human nature;
the other is responsive to contemporary social
demands. The one is independent of time,
place and circumstances; the other is adjusta-
ble to these various elements. The one represents a pedagogical constant; the other presents the widest margin of variation. The one
is generic in its embracement of all mankind;
the other is specific in its application to the
peculiar needs and requirements of each individual. Failure to grasp, with tight seizure,
this dual aim of education leads to much con-

fusion of thought and obfuscation of counsel
in our pedagogical discussions.

In the lower orders of creation the process,
in both of its aspects, is all but spontaneous.
The individual swiftly attains to the perfection of qualities, with little or no guidance and
direction, and acquires the requisite experience
and method, through the operation of instinct
which instantaneously hands down to each,
alike, the full patrimony of the race. With
man, this must be accomplished by the slower
and more uncertain processes of human pedagogy.

Education is not an end in itself, but is conditioned upon the nature of man and upon his
place in the social scheme; it is not an independent and self-contained entity, but is con-
ducive to the fulfilment of ulterior aims. The
pedagogical ideal and method will always depend upon the queries—"What is the chief end
of man?" and "What does society require of
him?"

Man as a Personality

The old idea of education derived its aim
from the conception of the origin and destiny
of man. Under this conception, man was regarded as the son of heaven—a creature made

a little lower than the angels, only that he might rise to the higher level by conscious effort. His present state and lot were regarded as a lapse from his pristine happiness, and his highest concern was to regain the blissful seat. Man was created in the image of God, Who breathed into his nostrils the breath of life, when he became a living soul. He was considered to be essentially a personality—a self-conscious, moral agent, who longed for the higher satisfaction of his nature, as the thirsty hart panteth for the water brook. The highest concern of this school of pedagogy was to develop man as a rational being—a creature capable of thinking, hoping, loving, believing, craving, striving for higher things. Shakespeare has given us perhaps the clearest definition from this point of view:

> "What a piece of work is man!
>   How noble in reason! how infinite in faculty!
>   In form and moving how express and admirable!
>   In action how like an angel!
>   In apprehension how like a God!"

History, philosophy and theology agreed substantially to this definition of man as the crown and climax of creation. The old definition of education, namely, "The process of unfolding the seed of immortality which God has im-

planted in men,'' was perfectly consistent with
this idea. However the form of statement
might be modified or multiplied, this was the
essential meaning which underlay them all.
The programs and subject matter of instruction were but incidental to this one controlling
purpose. Books, libraries, laboratories, sched-
ules, appliances, were but the scaffolding for
the structure. Discipline, culture, knowledge,
exact or refined, belles-lettres, poetry, music,
art, were all considered as incidental means of
developing in man the higher appreciation of
and reverence for himself as a conscious personality.

Man as an Instrumentality

Under the dominion of the Darwinian theory, the present day conception of man is that
he represents the higher section of biology,
rather than the direct descendant of heaven.
He is of the earth, earthy. In origin, development, purpose and destiny he is subject to the
same conditions as the beasts that perish. His
fundamental concern, therefore, is to provide
what he shall eat, what he shall drink, wherewithal he shall be clothed, and how he may derive creature comforts and temporary satisfaction as the days go by.

Under modern requirements, the demands of living make such a heavy draft upon human faculties that political economy, which Carlyle characterizes as a dismal science, is wont to embrace the entire sphere of social endeavor. The invention of machinery lies at the basis of modern industrial methods. The practical activities of the age are organized upon the basis of machinery in which the assembled parts coöperate in the accomplishment of the required task. Transition from the hand process to the factory process was made inevitable under the stimulus of inventive genius. The great industrial establishments of the modern world are as much a machine as a well built watch, in which all parts are incidental and coöperant to a single end. The human element is placed on the same footing as mechanical attachments. The individual, so far as he represents a conscious personality, is wholly submerged as a part of the machine to which he is attached. The contractor advertises for so many ''hands'' because the hand is often the only part of the individual called into requisition to accomplish the desired task. No demand is made upon the higher powers and faculties, and therefore they are wholly ignored in the designation. The term ''typewriter'' means either the machine which makes the impression upon paper, or the young woman who operates it. They are both considered as mere parts of the apparatus which transmits the author's thought to paper without modifying it. It is entirely conceivable that in the process of invention the human element in this psycho-physical process may be wholly eliminated. The stenographer, the telegraph operator, the printer, the messenger merely serve as mechanical mediaries, or pure instrumentalities, in the process of transmission of intelligence. The engineer, the brakeman, the mortorman, the chauffeur take their designation from their mechanical function. When we fly through the air on the limited express at the rate of sixty miles an hour, the engineer and the engine are alike but parts of the process of transportation. The "hello girl" who sits all day as part of the machinery of transmission of the human voice is but an attachment of the telephonic mechanism. Indeed, inventive genius has made the connective process automatic, so that the human element is no longer an indispensability. We need not, therefore, be surprised at the long standing feud between man and the machine. The working world has always opposed the invention of new machinery on the ground that it displaced the human element by mere mechanism. Man

is justly jealous of his human prerogative. In
the mere pronunciation of such words as "fire-
man," "salesman," "plowman," "workman,"
the penultimate accent plainly shows that the
function, and not the performer, receives the
stress of emphasis and consideration. Man
thus becomes a mere tool, or implement, in the
process of industrial advance. Human instrumentality is necessary to carry on the process
of the world's work. Agriculture, the mechanical activities, manufacture, trade and
transportation must be carried on through
such an agency or the social fabric must fail.
If, then, the exploitation of this side of man
must continue for all time to come, it is simply a matter of prudence to provide that he
should be made proficient as an instrument in
the performance of this mechanical mission.
Herein consist the basis and justification of
the modern claim for industrial education. If
man is, and of necessity must be, utilized as an
instrumentality in the production and distribution of wealth, then it is easy to conclude that
he should be trained to the highest degree of
efficiency in the accomplishment of such tasks.
Industrial education and occupational training
are hereby justified and made inevitable. The
captains of industry must be greatly concerned
in the perfecting of the tools, animate or in-

animate, that contribute to the efficient operation of their projects. The invention of a safety device or economic contrivance adds not so much to the efficiency of operation as improvement of their workmen as human instruments. As corporations have no souls, they have little regard for the higher personality of their work people. They can utilize on perfected instrumentalities. While it is true that life is more than meat, yet man must devote a large part of his powers to the procurement of meat; not for meat's sake, but in order that he might, through meat, attain to larger life. If meat and raiment were the end and aim of life, then man would needs be limited to an instrumentality to procure these things.

The old idea that man was a personality pure and simple disregarded almost wholly his incidental function as an instrumentality. In fact, man is of twofold nature. He is both instrumentality and personality. The two functions inhere in every human creature. Each represents complementary factors of a full development. The old idea, in order to escape the illogicality of its own philosophy, made of some men, the favored few, pure personalities; while the great bulk of mankind was worked to the lower level of beasts of burden, and was thus excluded from the highest sphere of human consideration. History in its records, even down to comparatively recent times, is concerned mainly with the deeds and doings of kings and noblemen, with persons of position and power and prestige. The people, in mass, had no voice or part in the process except as instruments to be utilized and exploited by the lordly pretensions of the higher class.

There is a constant duel between the process of machinery and the spirit of democracy— the one tending to subordinate the human element to the mechanical process; the other insisting upon the higher rights and powers of man. Democracy banishes distinction between classes, and gives all men the same right to develop and exploit the higher powers and susceptibilities with which they may be endowed. Our educational system to-day is between the upper and nether stress of these conflicting influences. If we keep clearly in mind the twofold development of man as an instrumentality and as a personality, we shall, thereby, get a clear understanding of the relative place and importance of the so-called practical and liberal education. The essential, immediate aim of industrial education is to develop man as an instrumentality. The chief end of the so-called liberal education is to develop man as a per-

sonality. These two features are not antagonistic nor mutually exclusive, but are joint
factors of a common product. The industrial
advocates would claim that their ultimate aim
is the development of man as a personality
through instrumentality. The higher education
presumes instrumentality as a corollary of personality.

The great bulk of mankind, even under the
best ordered conditions, are so circumstanced
that they are, perforce, compelled to devote
most of their time and strength as human tools.
The miner who must toil underground half of
the day, and thereby so exhaust his physical
energies that he must needs spend the other
half in recuperative rest, becomes almost as
much a tool of production as the pick he uses
to extract the coal from the ground. The ox
which pulls the plow and the plowman who
guides, or rather who follows it, are part and
partners in the general agricultural process. If,
however, the plowman leaves room for the
exercise of his human powers which transmute
the products of agriculture into higher values,
he thereby vindicates his claim to be lord of
creation. The man with the hoe aptly fulfills
this illustration:

"Bowed by the weight of centuries he leans
Upon his hoe and gazes on the ground:

The emptiness of ages in his face,
And on his back the burden of the world.
Who made him dead to rapture and despair?
Stolid, yet stunned, a brother to the ox."

This man with the hoe is of all men most miserable, unless, forsooth, he has a hope which bridges "the gulfs between him and the seraphim" and puts him *en rapport* with "Plato and the swing of the Pleiades, the long reaches of the peaks of song; the rift of dawn, the reddening of the rose." Unless, indeed, "this monstrous thing distorted and soul-quenched" can be touched with a quickening sense of personality, the ends of creation are defeated and we may as well welcome Thomas Huxley's friendly comet to blot mankind out of existence.

Under our present dispensation, most men must devote the larger part of their powers to processes of producing and distributing wealth, while a smaller number, either through natural or artificial selection, are set apart to the higher intellectual, moral, and spiritual tasks; but, however exacting the present necessities may be, it is incumbent upon each individual to have in view his best development as a personality.

The highest decree of the Godhead was— "Let us make man." The true end of education is to develop man, the average man, as a self-conscious personality. This can be done not by imparting information to the mind or facility to the fingers, but felicity to the feelings and inspiration to the soul. Develop the man; the rest will follow. The final expression of education is not in terms of discipline, culture, efficiency, service, or specific virtues, but in terms of manhood, which is the substance and summation of them all. The whole is greater than any of its parts.

When electricity has been developed and controlled, it can be given out in any desired form of manifestation. It may be transmuted into heat, light, tractive power or the more mysterious form resulting in ethereal transmission or the marvelous manifestation of the Roentgen rays. And so, when the manhood has been quickened, it may express itself in terms of character, efficiency, initiative, service or enjoyment, as that occasion may require. None of these things represent final values in themselves, but are incidental manifestations of manhood from which they are derived and to which they conduce.

CHARACTER

Character, as ordinarily defined, is the chief thing in our educational philosophy; but this is merely the mark, the image, the superscription, the impression from which to judge the inherent quality of the object upon which it is made. Manhood is the underlying substance which manifests itself through character. The sculptor cannot work as well on mud as on marble, because it lacks the inherent quality to hold and reflect the impression made upon it. Character is but the guinea's stamp; the man is the "gowd for a' that." Character issues from manhood as light from the sun or as fragrance from the flower.

Efficiency

The watchword of the practical world is "Efficiency." The economic application of effort to task is the industrial desideratum of the age. Under the slovenly system, half of the effort put forth is without beneficial effect. Efficiency consists in the economy of human energy in the accomplishment of personal or social tasks. It is an essential pedagogical fallacy to suppose that efficiency can be taught as an isolated quality. You must first develop the man before you can make a workman. The master and the man may wield the same instrument; the one proceeds with higher efficiency

because he has the vision to foresee the fruits
of his labor transmuted into higher human values. On the other hand, the man is a mere
eye-servant, whose vision cannot reach beyond
the time and the hour. The history of the
world emphasizes the disastrousness of this
fallacy. Labor, in order to be efficient, must be
directed to some ulterior end, namely, the ful-
fillment of the human aspirations of the laborer. In order that man may become an efficient instrumentality, he must first be developed as a conscious personality. Serfdom,
slavery and peonage, which seek to exploit man
as a purely mechanical or animal asset, are
shown to be a fatuous philosophy.

No human creature is ever at his best in any
field of endeavor unless he is quickened by a
conscious sense of his own individuality. For
this reason democracy is almost synonymous
with progress. To suppress the higher crav-
ings of a human being, in order to make of him
an easily controlled and contented instrument,
has been exploited and proved to be a self-
defeating policy. Slave labor is slothful labor.
Neither the slave, nor yet the semi-slave, can
compete in efficiency with the freeman; for the
one represents mindless muscle, while the other
represents muscle under the dominion of the
mind. Whenever the conscious sense of indi-

viduality is aroused in a single individual, a new power is added to the social equation. Any scheme of education which is focused upon specific educational preparation, without a broader basis of appeal, is as ineffectual as to substitute symptomatic for systematic treatment in therapeutics.

To make bricklayers men is a hundredfold more difficult than to make men bricklayers; for, if there be men, they will make bricks, even without straw, if bricks must needs be made. Consciousness of personality energizes all of the faculties and powers and gives them facility and adaptability as nothing else can do. The wise procedure is to develop personality, which easily results in efficient instrumentality.

Initiative

Elbert Hubbard, with Philistine philosophy, defines initiative as the ability to do the right thing without being told. It is the direct expression of manhood in terms of the thing which needs to be done. Manhood, therefore, perceiving the thing needful, proceeds to its accomplishment without exterior direction. If initiative is the ability to do the right thing, efficiency is the ability to do the thing right. Both of these flow from the common fountain.

Neither can be taught as isolated qualities, but both issue from the higher fountain of manhood.

SERVICE

Service, according to current cant, is considered the ultimate end of education. The whole drift of our educational scheme is tending in this direction; but the slightest reflection will convince the average intelligence that service is not an end in itself, but merely a means of developing the qualities of manhood on the part of those deprived of equal opportunity. The ultimate expression of service, therefore, is in terms of manhood. "Culture for service" has become a sing-song motto in our educational polity. Like all such mottoes, whose constant dinging wears off the fresh luster of the original significance, it has become sickled o'er with a pale cast of thought. If by culture we mean the perfection of human faculties, then the form of motto should be inverted so as to read "Service through culture." Experience proves that the developed personality not only becomes an effective instrumentality to meet its own personal needs of life, but will also utilize the larger powers to assist the less fortunate. Altruistic service justly receives

our highest meed of praise. The actuating
motive is the sure impulse of a highly developed personality to lift others to its own exalted plane of manhood. A prurient, eleemos-
ynary disposition, which merely obeys the
prevalent fashion or fancy, like the meritorious
almsgiving of the Pharisees, has its own reward. It was this superficial vicariousness
which the Apostle Paul deplored when he said,
"Though I give my substance to the poor and
my body to be burned, and have not love, I am
become as a tinkling cymbal and sounding
brass." True benevolence is the desire to
assist each of God's human creatures to develop his fullest personality. There is neither
natural satisfaction nor ultimate reward in
mere feeding the hungry and clothing the
naked. A little girl, dressing her doll-baby
alone, has a self-justifying delight in clothing
the naked, as the sausage grinder in the perpetual feeding process. Carlyle says, "That
anyone should die ignorant who had capacity
for knowledge is a tragedy." In order to
avert these human tragedies which are occurring all around us, the true man puts forth his
best endeavor that no one shall live or die
ignorant who has capacity for knowledge, or
vicious who has capacity for virtue, or sinful
who may receive the saving knowledge of the

truth. True manhood responds to the imperative force of the mandate, "Go ye into all the world and preach the gospel (of innate manhood), to every creature. He that believeth shall be saved and he that believeth not shall be damned." When these glad tidings are brought to the individual with the opportunity to embrace them, if he does not believe in his own essential manhood, deep down in the very cells and fibers of his nature, he is condemned already; nor is there any greater condemnation than this.

The missionary who cheerfully sacrifices every creature comfort in order that the humblest of human creatures may have the opportunity to develop the God-implanted norms of personality touches the highest level of true manhood. It is here that the motto, "Service through culture," finds the highest expression and justification.

ENJOYMENT

Just as electricity is not limited in its manifestation to heat and power alone, but sometimes gives itself out as light, so manhood cannot be confined in its outgivings to discipline or efficiency or sacrificial service, but at times and on occasions expresses itself in enjoyment and

in personal elation. It concerns itself as much
with things beautiful as with things useful or
with things good. The hard utilitarian and
vicarious theory of education is advocated only
by the self-denying or the unreflecting. Each
individual must spend a large fraction of his
time in pursuit of personal satisfaction, along
ways that are neither utilitarian nor vicarious.
Indeed, this is, perhaps, the highest outlet of
manhood; as the poet Whitman would say, it
is sufficient justification "to merely be."
Keenness of appreciation for intellectual, social, esthetic, moral and spiritual value is one
of the essential ends aimed at in education.
Faulty, indeed, would be that pedagogic scheme
which left this element out of account. Indeed,
on final analysis, the joy of service will be
found to be closely akin to other forms of personal gratification. Some of our educational
theories would educate people only for the factory and charity organizations. All else is regarded as selfish or unworthy gratification.
Banish from the world all literature, poetry,
music, art, architecture, and the beauties of
flowers, and the glories of the sky; take all
sculpture from the mantels and pictures from
the walls; put under ban the graces and
charms of pleasurable intercourse and social
satisfaction—and a man becomes a little more

than the wild savage of the forest. A comprehensive scheme of education, therefore, must give scope and play for exercise of the many-sided features of manhood. It must involve discipline, initiative, culture, personal and altruistic service and rational enjoyment.

The charge is often made that the so-called higher education has no direct practical aim. A sufficient response would be that its aim is to develop manhood. Merely this and nothing more. Manhood is its own justification and needs no ulterior policy or sanction. When this is developed, as we have already seen, it readily transmutes itself into the requisite mode of manifestation, whether it be efficiency, initiative, culture, vicarious service, or the joy of existence.

Someone asked a New Englander what did they grow in the rocky hills of that barren section. The quick reply was, "We grow men here." New England has, indeed, been the breeding ground for men. This manhood has manifested itself at times in industry, as seen in the exploitation of the resources of this continent. Wherever you see a railroad or a factory or any of the gigantic business and industrial organizations which characterize our economic system, the underlying basis can easily be traced back to New England manhood.

Hill, Rockefeller, Morgan, Harriman are examples of this manhood devoting itself to the making of money; in Emerson, Longfellow, Lowell, Russell we see the same manhood transmuting itself into culture; Edison and Morse devote their powers to the unraveling of the mysteries of nature; Garrison, Phillips and Sumner express their manhood in terms of moral and social reforms; Howard, Armstrong, Cravath and Ware express it in terms of altruistic service; but there is the self-same manhood that worketh in all and through all.

It can be seen that human values are but the various outgivings of manhood. Man is more than industry, trade, commerce, politics, government, science, art, literature or religion, all of which grow out of his inherent needs and necessities. The fundamental aim of education, therefore, should be manhood rather than mechanism. The ideal is not a working man, but a man working; not a business man, but a man doing business; not a school man, but a man teaching school; not a statesman, but a man handling the affairs of state; not a medicine man, but a man practising medicine; not a clergyman, but a man devoted to the things of the soul.

Application to the Colored Race

In the foregoing discussion I have laid down the general proposition disengaged from the meshes of racial incidents. It now remains to point out their pertinency to the present situation and circumstances of the colored race of the United States.

We must keep clearly in mind that the educational process is always under domination of contemporary opinion. The education prescribed for any class is likely to be conditioned upon the presumed relationship of that class to the social body. When woman was regarded as an inferior creature, whose destiny was to serve as a tool and plaything of man, she was accorded only such education as would fit her for this subsidiary function. Any other training was regarded as unnecessary and mischievous. It is only within comparatively recent times, when man began to realize the essential human quality and powers of the female sex, and deemed it not mockery to place her on the same footing with himself, that the comprehensive education of woman has become a possibility.

The traditional relation of the American negro to the society of which he forms a part is too well known to need extensive treatment in this connection. The African slave was introduced into this country as a pure animal instrumentality to perform the rougher work under dominion of his white lord and master. There was not the remotest thought of his human personality. No more account was taken of his higher qualities than of the higher susceptibilities of the lower animals. His mission was considered to be as purely mechanical as that of the ox which pulls the plough. Indeed, his human capabilities were emphatically denied. It was stoutly contended that he did not possess a soul to be saved in the world to come nor a mind to be enlightened in the world that now is. Under the dominion of this dogma, education was absolutely forbidden him. It became a crime even to attempt to educate this *tertium quid,* which was regarded as little more than brute and little less than human. The white race, in its arrogant conceit, constituted the personalities and the negroes the instrumentalities. Man may be defined as a distinction-making animal. He is ever prone to set up barriers between members of his own species and to deny one part of God's human creatures the inalienable birthright vouchsafed to all alike. But the process was entirely logical and consistent with the prevailing philosophy.

Northern Philanthropy

The anti-slavery struggle stimulated the moral energy of the American people in a manner that perhaps has never had a parallel in the history of vicarious endeavor. "One touch of nature makes the whole world kin." In dealing with fundamental principles of human rights and human wrongs involved in the issue of slavery, these moral reformers found that the negro was a human being, endowed with heart and mind and conscience like themselves; albeit these powers of personality had long been smothered and imbruted by centuries of suppression and hard usage. These philanthropists believed in the essential manhood of the negro. This belief was the chief dynamic of their endeavor. Upon this foundation they not only broke the negro's chain, but clothed him with political and civic prerogative as an American citizen. They established schools and colleges and universities for him because they believed in his higher susceptibilities. To-day we are almost astounded at the audacity of their faith. They projected a scheme of education comparable with the standards set up for the choicest European youth for a race which had hitherto been submerged below the zero point of intelligence. These schools and colleges, founded and fostered on this basis, were the beginning of the best that there is in the race and the highest which it can hope to be.

But, alas, as the passion engendered by the war grew weaker and weaker, the corresponding belief in the negro has also declined, and the old dogma concerning his mission as a human tool has begun to reassert itself. In certain sections the white race has always claimed that the negro should not be encouraged in the development of personality. The denial of the designation "mister" is suggestive of this disposition. With them the term "mister" is made to mean a direct designation of personality. There is no objection to such titles as "doctor," "reverend" or "professor," as these connote professional rather than personal quality.

Our whole educational activities are under the thrall of this retrograde spirit. We are marking time rather than moving forward. The work is being carried on rather than up. Our bepuzzled pedagogs are seriously reflecting over the query, *Cui bono?*—Is it worth while? Few, indeed, are left who have the intensity of belief and the intrepidity of spirit to defend the higher pretensions of the negro without apology or equivocation. The old form

of appeal has become insipid and uninspiring.
The ear has become dull to its dinning. The
old blade has become blunt and needs a new
sharpness of point and keenness of edge.
Where now is heard the tocsin call whose key-
note a generation ago resounded from the
highlands of Kentucky and Tennessee to the
plains of the Carolinas calling the black youths,
whose hopes ran high within their bosoms, to
rise and make for higher things? This clarion
note, though still for the nonce, shall not become a lost chord. Its inspiring tones must
again appeal to the youth to arise to their
higher assertion and exertion. If you wish to
reach and inspire the life of the people, the approach must be made not to the intellect,
nor yet to the feelings, as the final basis of
appeal, but to the manhood that lies back of
these. That education of youth, especially the
suppressed class, that does not make insistent
and incessant appeals to the smothered manhood (I had almost said godhood) within will
prove to be but vanity and vexation of spirit.
What boots a few chapters in Chemistry, or
pages in History, or paragraphs in Philosophy,
unless they result in an enlarged appreciation
of one's own manhood? Those who are to
stand in the high places of intellectual, moral
and spiritual leadership of such a people in

such a time must be made to feel deep down
in their own souls their own essential manhood.
They must believe that they are created in the
image of God and that nothing clothed in human guise is a more faithful likeness of that
original. This must be the dominant note in
the education of the negro. If the note itself
is not new, there must at least be a newness of
emphasis and insistence. The negro must learn
in school what the white boy learns from association and environment. The American white
man in his ordinary state is supremely conscious of his manhood prerogative. He may be
ignorant or poor or vicious; yet he never for-
gets' that he is a man. But every feature of
our civilization is calculated to impress upon
the negro a sense of his inferiority and to make
him feel and believe that he is good for nothing
but to be cast out and trodden under foot of
other men. A race, like an individual, that
compromises its own self-respect paralyzes
and enfeebles its own energies. The motto
which should be engraved upon the conscience
of every American negro is that which Milton
places in the mouth of His Satanic Majesty:
"The mind is its own place and of itself can
make a heaven of hell; a hell of heaven." To
inculcate this principle is the highest mission
of the higher education. The old theologians

used to insist upon the freedom of the will, but the demand of the negro to-day is the freedom and independence of his own spirit. Destroy this and all is lost; preserve it, and though political rights, civil privileges, industrial opportunities be taken away for the time, they will all be regained.

By the development of manhood on the part of the negro nothing is farther from my thought than the inculcation of that pugnacious, defiant disposition which vents itself in wild ejaculations and impotent screaming against the evils of society. I mean the full appreciation of essential human qualities and claims, and the firm, unyielding determination to press forward to the mark of this high calling, and not to be swerved from its pursuit by doubt, denial, danger, rebuff, ridicule, insult and contemptuous treatment. While the negro may not have it within his power to resist or overcome these things, he must preserve the integrity of his own soul.

The higher education of the negro up to this point has been very largely under the direction and control of philanthropy. The support has come almost wholly from that source. The development of this sense of manhood should be the highest concern of a wise, discriminating philanthropy, for if this is once developed the

negro will be able to handle his own situation
and relieve his philanthropic friends from further consideration or concern; but, if he fails
to develop this spirit of manhood, he will be
but a drag upon the resources of philanthropy
for all time to come.

The negro must develop courage and self-
confidence. A grasp upon the principles of
knowledge gives the possessor the requisite
spirit of confidence. To the timid, the world
is full of mystery manipulated and controlled
by forces and powers beyond their ken to comprehend. But knowledge convinces us that
there is no mystery in civilization. The railroad, the steamship and the practical projects
that loom so large to the unreflecting are but
the result of the application of thought to
things. The mechanical powers and forces of
nature are open secrets for all who will under-
take to unravel the mystery. And so it is with
essential and moral principles. The one who
would have himself rooted and grounded in the
fundamental principles of things can look with
complacence upon the panorama of the world's
progress. The negro should plant one foot on
the Ten Commandments and the other on the
Binomial Theorem: he can then stand stead-
fast and immovable, however the rain of racial

wrath may fall or the angry winds of prejudice may blow and beat upon him.

The educated negro must learn to state his own case and to plead his own cause before the bar of public opinion. No people who raise up from out their midst a cultivated class, who can plead their own cause and state their own case, will fail of a hearing before the just judgment of mankind.

The educated negro to-day represents the first generation grown to the fullness of the stature of manhood under the influence and power of education. They are the first ripened fruit of philanthropy, and by them alone will the wisdom or folly of that philanthropy be justified. The hope of the race is focused in them. They are the headlight to direct the pathway through the dangers and vicissitudes of the wilderness. For want of vision, the people perish. For want of wise direction, they stumble and fall. There is no body of men in the world to-day, nor in the history of the world, who have, or ever have had, greater responsibilities or more coveted opportunities than devolve upon the educated negro to-day. It is, indeed, a privilege to be a negro of light and leading in such a time as this. The incidental embarrassments and disadvantages which for the time being must be endured are not to be compared with the far more exceeding weight of privileges and glory which awaits him if he rises to these high demands. For such a privilege well may he forego the pleasure of civilization for a season.

His world consists of ten million souls, who have wrapped up in them all of the needs and necessities, powers and possibilities of human nature; they contain all of the norms of civilization, from its roots to its florescence. His is the task to develop and vitalize these smothered faculties and potentialities. His education will prove to be but vanity and vexation of spirit, unless it ultimates in this task. He is the salt of the earth, and, if the salt lose its savor, wherewith shall it be salted? If the light within the racial world be darkness, how great is that darkness?

The highest call of the civilization of the world of to-day is to the educated young men of the belated races. The educated young manhood of Japan, China, India, Egypt, Turkey must lift their own people up to the level of their own high conception. They must partake of the best things in the civilization of Europe and show them unto their own people. The task of the educated American negro is the same as theirs, intensified, perhaps, by the more difficult and intricate tangle of circumstances and conditions with which he has to deal.

He cannot afford to slink into slothful satisfaction and enjoy a tasteless leisure or with inane self-deception hide his head under the shadows of his wings, like the foolish bird, which thereby hopes to escape the wrath to come. The white race, through philanthropy, has done much; but its vicarious task culminated when it developed the first generation of educated men and women. They must do the rest. These philanthropists spoke for us when our tongues were tied. They pleaded our cause when we were speechless; but now our faculties have been unloosed. We must stand upon our own footing. In buffeting the tempestuous torrents of the world we must either swim on the surface or else sink out of sight. The greatest gratitude that the beneficiary can show to the benefactor is, as soon as possible, to do without his benefaction. The task of race statesmanship and reclamation devolves upon the educated negro of this day and generation. Moral energy must be brought to bear upon the task, whether the negro be engaged in the production of wealth or in the more recondite pursuits which minister to the higher needs of man.

The white race is fast losing faith in the

negro as an efficient and suitable factor in the
equation of our civilization. Curtailment of
political, civil and religious privilege and opportunity is but the outward expression of this
apostasy. As the white man's faith decreases,
our belief in ourselves must increase. Every
negro in America should utter this prayer, with
his face turned toward the light: "Lord, I
believe in my own inherent manhood; help
Thou my unbelief." The educated negro must
express his manhood in terms of courage, in
the active as well as in the passive voice: courage to do, as well as to endure; courage to con-
tend for the right while suffering wrong; the
courage of self-belief that is always commensurate with the imposed task. The world believes in a race that believes in itself; but
justly despises the self-bemeaned. Such is the
mark,—such is the high calling to which the
educated negro of to-day is called. May he rise
to the high level of it. Never was there a field
whiter unto harvest; never was there louder
cry for laborers in the vineyard of the Lord.

CRIME AMONG NEGROES

The criminal status of the negro race is a matter that should be carefully weighed and investigated, and cautious and reasoned conclusion deduced therefrom. The anti-negro doctrinaires are ever prone to seize upon the surface appearance of things criminal and utilize them to blacken and blast the reputation of the race.

The census of 1890 made a study of criminal statistics. Although the Twelfth Census made no such investigation, there was a special bulletin issued in 1904, which made a partial examination of criminal statistics.

The one essential fact, so far as the negro race is concerned, is that twelve per cent. of the population contributed thirty-two per cent. of the crimes of the United States. This ratio was practically the same for 1890 and 1904. During the interval of fourteen years there has been no absolute increase in negro crime, but in some instances there was a relative increase, as compared with that of the white population.

In 1890 there were 24,227 negro prisoners in the United States. In 1904 there were 26,870 such prisoners. Although there was some discrepancy in the methods of return at the two census periods, the underlying fact remains that the criminal status of the race had made no notable increase, as compared with the growth of the negro population during the intervening fourteen years.

The sociologist first ascertains the facts. Then he accounts for and interprets them. Finally, he generalizes upon them and points out their prophetic import. The orator, on the other hand, first generalizes and prophesies, and afterwards finds it necessary to ascertain the facts lying at the basis of his generalization and prophecy. Now the fact is that the negro has a criminal record about three times as great as his numbers entitle him to. How shall we account for this? If one should go to England or to any other part of the earth and study the condition of the people who live in poverty in the crowded cities, he would find an overwhelming preponderance of crime among the submerged elements as compared with the general population. The negro shows this high criminal rating because he constitutes, in the United States and especially in the large cities, the submerged stratum where the bulk of actionable crime is found the world over. Crime is a question of condition, not of color.

Another reason, in my judgment, which contributes to the seeming increase in negro crime is the fact that during the last fifteen years there has grown up, on the part of the white race, a spirit of racial exclusiveness and intolerance. This is outwardly manifested in the public provisions for the sharp separation of the races in all matters where there is likely to be anything like intimacy of contact. Formerly there was a kindly personal and patriarchal relation between the races, but in these latter days it is becoming hard and business like. "If the negro offends against the law, let him perish by the law," is the prevailing motto and method. A famous English writer some time ago said: "If you wish to destroy a feeble race, you can do so more easily by the law than without it. Make the laws as rigid as possible and enforce them rigidly." Those who watch events closely must have noticed the application of this principle in certain parts of the country.

I believe, from observation and examination, that, taking the Southern courts as a whole, the negro in some cases is treated unusually severely, and in others with unusual lenity. Balancing the two extremes, he gets substantial justice; but there is a difference between fairness and justice. *Fairness* consists in equal distribution of favor; *justice* in equal application of rights. The laborer in the parable, who entered at the eleventh hour, was received on terms of compensatory equality with the one who had borne the heat and burden of the day, but the more strenuous workman could not accuse the master of the vineyard of injustice, but merely of unfairness. If the negro gets justice in the Southern courts, the white man gets less than justice, and this makes an unfair distribution of penalties.

When negroes commit crimes among themselves they are not apt to be punished with undue severity, but when they commit crime against the white race punishment is sure, swift and severe. On the other hand, when the white man commits an offense against the negro, acquittal is almost sure to follow; and even if convicted he is released with a slight fine and does not go to swell the prison record of his race. Even where the white man commits an offence against his own race he is not apt to receive the full rigor of the law. When two races are living together, the race which assumes superiority is wont to regard itself as sacred in the eyes of the other, and is very reluctant to humiliate any of its members, even by due process of law.

I believe that all will agree that a white person in Massachusetts is in every way as upright and as well behaved as the white person in any other place in the world, and yet, if we follow statistics, we find that the white people in Mississippi are angels of grace as compared with the white people of Massachusetts. In Massachusetts there are 5,477 whites in prison; in Mississippi only 114. The ingenuity of the Yankee sociologist can easily explain away this seeming discrepancy. By the same process of reasoning, the glaring criminal discrepancy between the races can be accounted for. There are probably no more white prisoners in Massachusetts than there ought to be, but no man in his senses, not even Senator Vardaman, will claim that only 114 white persons in Mississippi should be "in durance vile." By parity of reason, it is fair to say that probably in the South the number of white prisoners falls immensely below the number of white offenders against the law.

If the entire negro population should withdraw from the South and its place be supplied by whites occupying a similar status, the crime rate of the South would *not* be appreciably affected. In the United States as a whole there is an average of one prisoner to every .one thousand of the population. In the South Atlantic states, where the negro is found in the largest numbers, the criminal rate is almost exactly the same as that of the nation at large. In the North Atlantic states, where there are few negroes, there is a still higher average, and in the Western states, where there are no negroes, comparatively speaking, the rate is highest of all. It is impossible to trace any connection between race and crime. If the negro in the North shows a much higher criminal rate than the negro in the South, it is also true that the white race in the North shows a greater ratio of crime over that same race in the South.

The negro in this country is the sacrificial race. He is the burden bearer of the white race. He constitutes the mud sill of society and suffers the ills of that lowly place. He performs the rough work of society. He suffers the affliction and even commits the crimes which always fall to the lot of his status. Were it not for him the white race would suffer corresponding ills. The Caucasian should appreciate the vicariousness of the black man's lot and not strive by false reasoning and force argument to make his burdens greater than they are.

Just as the negro death rate, three times as great as that of the whites, is clearly due to his condition, so his crime rate, bearing the same disproportion, is also attributable to the same cause.

What should be the attitude of negro men and women of light and learning toward this high criminal record and the interpretation just placed upon it? In the first place, they should strive insistently and incessantly to reduce this rate. It is always more satisfactory, from a sociological point of view, to remove an evil than to explain the cause of its existence. Laws are made for the protection of the weak. It makes my heart bleed when I see a negro violating the law, which is his only safeguard and protection under our scheme of civilization. This Samsonian folly pulls down the pillars of the temple of justice, the only asylum for the weak. Colored men should use their best offices to persuade those who are in control of the lawmaking agencies in the States and in the nation to enact only such laws as can be cheerfully upheld and obeyed by all, without compromise of becoming dignity and self-respect. The white race should enact laws of such equity and fairness that the negroes will have no cause to complain of their unrighteousness and injustice. For if the laws themselves are unrighteous, where shall we look for righteousness?

Let the negro obey the Ten Commandments and the white man the Golden Rule. Then all will be well. Ephraim will not envy Judah, and Judah will not vex Ephraim.

THE AMERICAN NEGRO AS A POLITICAL FACTOR

Professor E. A. Freeman once defined politics as present history, and history as past politics. With a greater proneness for picturesque language, John J. Ingalls described politics as "the metaphysics of force," in which none but the strenuous may expect to play a part. According to Webster's Dictionary, politics is "that part of ethics which has to do with the regulation and government of a nation or state, the defense of its existence and rights against foreign control and conquest, the augmentation of its strength and resources, and the protection of its citizens in their rights, with the preservation and improvement of their morals." According to this conception, it will be seen that politics is the chief concern of man in his associated relations, and conditions all other modes of activity, whether economic, industrial, educational or social.

The derivative, or secondary, meaning of

the word "politics" is the management of a political party and the advancement of candidates to office. Throughout our discussion it will be well to keep sharply in mind the distinction between politics as the science of government and politics as the art of partisan policy and manipulation. In a country like ours, where the functions of government are conducted through partisan organizations, the secondary meaning of the word is apt to obscure its primary significance in popular estimation. The vast majority of the people have no conception of the word aside from party contentions and the procurement of office. So great is the perversity of popular understanding that to refer to a public man as a politician is accounted an uncomplimentary designation.

In considering the negro as a political factor, reference is hardly ever had to the essential functions and purposes of government, but he is regarded merely as the sport, the jest and the riddle of party rivalry. Our political philosophers are inclined to ignore the negro as a constituent governmental factor by reason of the manner of his introduction into this country. The African was imported for the sole purpose of performing manual and menial labor. His bodily powers alone were called into requisition. His function was as purely

mechanical as that of the ox which pulls the
plow. He was a chattel, a part of the nation's material assets. There was no more
thought of admitting him into the body politic
than of thus ennobling the lower animals. The
gulf that separated him from the proud Aryan
was supposed to be so wide and deep that the
two races could never be made amenable to
the same moral, political and social *régime*.

But the transplanted African has manifested surprising capacities and aptitudes for
the standards of his European captors, so that
the races must now be separated, if at all, by
purely artificial barriers. This upward struggle on the part of the African has been against
continuous doubt, ridicule and contemptuous
denial on the part of those who would profit
by his inferior status. Those who once assumed the piety of their day and generation
at one time stoutly declared that the negro did
not possess a soul to be saved in the world to
come, but was merely as the beasts that perish;
but he is now considered the man of oversoul,
as Emerson would say, by reason of his marvelous emotional characteristics. Then the
wise ones maintained that he did not possess a
mind to be enlightened according to the standards of European intellect, and hence he was
forbidden a knowledge of letters. The same

dogma affirmed that the black man would not work except under the stern compulsion of the white man's beneficent whip, and that he would die out under freedom. But all of these dogmas have been disproved by the progress of events.

The ancient doctrine of racial inferiority, however, now reasserts itself under a different guise. With a prudent generality it avers with great vehemence of spirit that the negro is inherently, unalterably and everlastingly inferior to the white race as a part of God's cosmic scheme of things, and, therefore, is an unfit factor for self-government, which is the highest human function. It is a shrewd and cunning controversialist who posits the universal negative and defies the world to disprove his thesis. His tactical method is to deny all things, and to ignore that which has been proved. But, in spite of it all, the negro is steadily and unmistakably moving toward the great free ocean of human privilege, and, like the mountain stream, though his progress here and there may be impeded and delayed, artificial barriers and obstructions can only retard but not stay his onward flow.

The white race in this country is ensnared in meshes of its own law. The negro has been, and is, the incidental beneficiary of this entanglement. Circumstances have forced him into a political scheme not designed for him. Universal principles have no ethnic quality. By the irony of history the white man's maxims have risen up to trouble him. The Ten Commandments will not budge, neither will the Declaration of Independence. It is said that the Anglo-Saxon race is noted for its bad logic, but good sense. The revolutionary fathers must have shut their eyes to the logical results of their own doctrine, or else they lacked the courage of their conscience. The negro has been the incidental beneficiary of the two waves of revolutionary feeling which have swept the current of popular sentiment beyond the limits of its accustomed channel. He moves up and down on the scale of national sentiment as the mercury in the thermometric tube, reaching blood-heat in periods of national stress and excitement and sinking to the freezing point in seasons of tranquillity and repose. In none other than revolutionary crises could the Declaration of Independence have been written or the last two amendments appended to our Federal Constitution. The former held out to the negro the hope of ultimate citizenship and political equality, while the latter was the first step toward this realization. These two milestones of promise and partial fulfilment were one hundred years apart. As the nation is becoming settled in its normal modes, the disposition is to relegate the negro to the state of political nullity.

But, despite this political apostasy, the negro constitutes a political factor which cannot be ignored without local and national peril. He constitutes one-ninth the numerical strength of the American people, and is promiscuously scattered over the whole geographical area of the United States, ranging in relative density from ten to one in the black belts of the South to less than one per cent. in the higher latitudes. He furnishes one-sixth of the wage-earning class, and is inextricably interwoven in the national, industrial, and economic fabric. He speaks the same language, conducts the same modes of activity, reads the same literature, worships God after the same ritual as his white fellow citizens. As the late Dr. W. T. Harris once said, he has acquired the Anglo Saxon consciousness and put on his spiritual clothing. He delights in his new habiliment. He appeals to his white brother in the language of Ruth to Naomi: "Where thou goest I will go; and where thou lodgest I will lodge; thy people shall be my people, and thy God my God; where thou diest I will die, and there will I be buried."

A nation consists of the people living in a prescribed territory who hold the same general belief, sentiment and aspiration. The negro is, therefore, not an alien, but an essential part of the body politic. He is not like the Red Indian, with whose corporeal presence alone we have to deal and who stands stolidly aloof from the great throbbing current of national thought, feeling and aspirations, but he is a vital part in the spirit and potency of the national life. The negro is not merely a recipient, but a partaker in all of the objects and aims of government. Is he not a vital element in every measure intended to preserve the national peace and prosperity, to augment the nation's strength and resources, for the protection of citizens in their rights, and the preservation and improvement of their morals? The negro may indeed be eliminated by force as a factor in party management and patronage, but he can no more be eliminated from politics, in the broader significance of that term, than we can eliminate one side from a triangle without destroying the figure.

In current political discussion the negro is ever referred to as a negligible public quantity. The term "southern people," by a strange twist of lexical usage, is intended to signify a part, and sometimes a smaller part, of the community, and yet the negro in the South, in some instances, constitutes the majority of the population and contributes the greater part of the industrial strength, and makes possible the larger proportion of the public powers and functions of the State. Whenever political exigency suggests the curtailment of the representative power resident in the black population by way of reducing representation in the national congress, the beneficiaries of this power interpose the most strenuous and vehement objections. The marble apex of a monument may indeed look with despite upon the grosser material of its foundation, but it cannot deny that the foundation is as essential an element of the structure as its more ornamental and pretentious capstone.

The present reactionary political tendency has produced a class of political leaders who base their motive on race hatred and strife. They are adepts in the use of the dynamic power of race animosity. Without philosophic insight or far-seeing wisdom, they appeal to the passion of their followers with utter recklessness of logic and conscience. That the negro is incapable of self-government is a maxim which springs spontaneously from the lips of every speaker and to the pen tip of every

writer who attempts to justify the unrighteous
and iniquitous political treatment which is accorded him. This assertion they relish and
roll under their tongues as a sweet morsel.
By hoary usage and glib recital it has become
a stereotyped motto. We are ever referred to
the failure of the native tribes in Africa, the
dismal experiments of Hayti and Liberia, and
the reconstruction régime of the Southern
States. These are always recounted in the
same order of recital, and set forth with the
same vehemence of rhetoric as the basis of the
same derogatory conclusion. The argument,
or alleged argument, has been repeated so often
that the indolent feel forced to accept it
through sheer weariness. It is dinned into
their dull understanding by unending and
never-varying repetition as the recurrent
chorus of a popular song. The unvaried repetition of hoary argument ordinarily damages
the intellectual reputation of its users as being
deficient in originality and resource; but those
who delight to belittle and condemn the negro are no whit abashed by such considerations
of moral and intellectual frugality.

What is self government? If by the power
of self-government we mean the ability of any
people to exist according to the requirements
of their stage of development under their own

autonomy, and to adjust themselves to that environment, then all of the people on the face of the earth are capable of self-government. If, on the other hand, it implies that the ability of the retarded races to regulate their affairs after the fashion of the most advanced section of the European people, then the question is not only unnecessary but preposterous. Ireland has for years been waging a gigantic struggle for the priceless boon of self-government, as the Englishman understands and exercises that function, but England, on the other hand, is determined to withhold it on the ground that the wild, hysteric Celt is not prepared to exercise so high a prerogative with safety to himself and to the British Empire. The masses of the population of Europe, with centuries of inherited freedom and civilization behind them, are not deemed fit for self-government in the exalted sense of that term. Indeed, it is only the Anglo-Saxon race that has as yet demonstrated the capacity to use this prerogative as a means of social and political progress. The revolutions and counter revolutions and rumors of revolutions which are almost daily occurring in South and Central American Republics show that the forms of government copied from Anglo-Saxon models are far in advance of the development of these

Latin copyists. Self-government is not an absolute but a relative term. The Red Indian governed himself for centuries before the advent of the pale-face, and throve much better under his own autonomy than under alien control. The negroes of Hayti under their own form of government are as happy and contented, as thrifty and progressive, and are approaching the standards of European civilization as surely and as rapidly as the corresponding number of blacks in Jamaica under British control, or as a like number of negroes in Georgia under the dominion of the Stars and Stripes. If it be true that the negro has never shown any conspicuous capacity for self-government after the European standard, it is also true that the white race has not yet shown any conspicuous success in governing him.

The Republic of Hayti, contrary to prevailing belief, is the most marvelous illustration of self-governing ability on the face of the globe. Where else can be found a race of slaves who rose up in their independence of spirit and banished the ruling race to another continent, set up free government, and maintained it for one hundred years in face of the taunts and sneers and despiteful usage of a frowning world? If there be imperfections, internal dissensions, and repeated revolutions, it is merely a repetition of the experience of mankind in learning the lesson of self-government.

Liberia is held up to ridicule and scorn, and pointed to as an everlasting argument of the negro's governmental incapacity; and yet we have here a handful of ex-slaves who had only played for a while in the backyard of American civilization, and who, feeling the fires of freedom burning in their breasts, crossed the ocean and establishehd a government on the miasmatic coasts of Africa. This government has been maintained, however, feebly, for ninety years. For nearly a century a handful of American negroes have exercised a salutary control over two millions of natives, and have maintained themselves amid the intrigue and sinister design of great European powers. If the colony at Jamestown or at Plymouth had been forced to confront such an overwhelming number of savages as the Liberian colony has had to do, and had they been cut off from the constant stream of European reinforcement, sympathy and support fifty years after their foundation, they would have perished from savage onslaught and the vicissitudes of the wilderness of the new world.

But those who deny the political capacity

of the negro point to the reconstruction régime, and exclaim, "What need we of further
proof?" At the time of reconstruction ninety-
five per cent. of the negroes were densely illiterate, none of whom had had experience in
governmental affairs. This happened, too, at
a period of general political and social up-
heaval, when the country was overrun with
nondescript and renegade adventurers who
were going throughout the land seeking whom
they might devour. They seized upon the
newly enfranchised negro as their natural prey.
And yet these ignorant ex-slaves, amid all the
snares which beset them from without and
within, maintained governments for several
years, against which the only charge that has
ever been preferred is that they were grotesque
and extravagant. Grotesqueness is a matter
of taste. In many minds it is synonymous
with the unusual. If we are unaccustomed to
seeing negroes in places of political control,
the spectacle of the negro congressman or
judge would at first seem incongruous and
grotesque, but as a part of the usual order it
would become normal and seemly in our eyes.
If we may believe the rumors of municipal
mismanagement, it is doubtful whether any of
the Southern States, in their palmiest reconstruction days, could equal New York, Phil-

adelphia, San Francisco, or St. Louis in the quality or extent of public corruption. The corrupting influence and practice, be it understood, were not due to the initiative of the negro, but of the white carpetbagger and native scalawag who exploited him in his weakness. These much-abused "negro governments," as they are called, changed the oligarchy of the conquered States into true democracies, inaugurated a system of public instruction for all classes, and the general character of their constitutions was regarded as so excellent that many of them have not been altered up to the present time, except for the worse. As documents of human liberty they stand out bold and pronounced as compared with the tricky instruments that have supplanted them. They passed no laws against human liberty, or at variance with the Constitution of the United States. They denied no man the God given right of liberty, or the constitutionally vouchsafed privilege of participating in the government under which he must live. The failure of these governments was inevitable. To expect ignorant and inexperienced slaves to maintain a government not merely for themselves, but also for a greater number of Anglo-Saxons with trained faculty for leadership and inborn power of dominion, is a proposition too preposterous for the present generation to entertain. The marvel is not that they succeeded so poorly, but that they proceeded at all. It is not to the negro's discredit that he did not accomplish the impossible.

It is time to lay aside the animosities of bygone reconstruction and consider the situation in the light of changed conditions. The question of the present day is not whether the negro can govern himself, but how far, with increasing intelligence and substance, he can co-operate with the white race in maintaining good government for all; and whether he can be effectually ignored as a governmental factor by any section of the country without accumulating serious peril, not only for that section, but for the nation at large.

That the participation of the negro in governmental affairs constitutes a menace both to himself and the community is a dogma which has attained wide currency and general acceptance in present day discussion; but, like other damaging dogmas of which he from time immemorial has been made the victim, this proposition is not justly upheld by facts or argument; and yet it has been proclaimed or asseverated with such positiveness of assertion and rhetorical vehemence as almost to deceive his erstwhile friends, who once championed his

cause as being entitled to the full measure of
the prerogative and privilege of an American
citizen. The former enthusiastic and aggressive attitude toward the rights of this race
has given way to a feeble, apathetic and apol-
ogetic avowal of faith in the abstract principle
of human rights, but there is a sinister indifference to practical application and concrete
sanction. Such defenders of the negro's cause

> Damn with faint praise, assent with civil leer:
> And without sneering teach the rest to sneer.

This radical change of attitude has been due
to a studied and deliberate policy on the part
of the more rabid and rancorous anti-negro
agitators, who study to make this race odious
and offensive in the eyes of the civilized world.
They have seized upon the evil deeds of the
dastardly wrongdoer, and exploited them to the
everlasting detriment of a whole race. Their
chief delight consists in learning that some negro, in some part of the land, has committed
a flagrant and outrageous crime. They count
that day a sad one when the morning's paper
does not reveal that some one out of ten millions has been apprehended for a grave and
nefarious offense. With ghoulish glee they
revel in the hideous manifestations of human

nature if the culprit happens to be of the despised blood.

Such a deliberate and calculated propaganda to exploit and magnify the moral and criminal imperfections of any other element of our population would blast and blacken the reputation of the race held in despite, and make it odious in the estimation of their fellow-men. If every offense committed by an Italian wrongdoer should be magnified in its heinous and hideous features, and proclaimed in flaming headlines all over America as portraying the bestial traits and tendencies of the diabolical "dago," that race would soon be deemed unfit to form a constituent and participating factor in the equation of national life. The negro race is daily subjected to microscopic search for shortcomings and imperfections to be exploited for political ends. The negro is the victim of the iniquitous propaganda that portrays and magnifies repugnant imperfections which in the case of other races are attributed to human frailty. This political philosophy is clearly expressed in one of the homely maxims of its chief philosopher: "The negro is a frozen serpent, and we propose to keep him frozen." His facts are erroneous and his philosophy is false. The negro is in no sense a menace to America or to any part of it except in so far as igno-

rance is a menace to knowledge, vice to virtue,
degradation to decency; and the only effective
way to relieve the menace of the situation is by
removing the cause and not perpetuating it
under the spell of any fancied dread. If the
negro is to be kept "frozen" under such frenzied philosophy, the white race, too, may become frost-bitten by the resulting frigidity of
the atmosphere.

On the other hand, the negro has evinced
amazing patriotic devotion. As soon as the
first pangs of grief at severance from his native land faded away, he fell completely in love
with his new environment. He soon forgot
the "sunny clime and palmy wine" of his native land for the "cotton, corn and sweet po-
tatoes" of old Virginia. The negro is unsur-
passed in the strength and intensity of his local
attachment. Herein consists the true quality
of patriotism. It is not to be found merely in
the achievements of renowned warriors and
statesmen, which indeed are their own reward.
In this sense only a few conspicuous names in
any country could be accounted patriotic, but
rather the duties and endearments of the common people make the deeper and more lasting
impression upon the human heart. Robert
Burns, the national poet of Scotland, has
seized upon the endearments and local attach-

ments of the lowly life of Scotland and woven
them into soulful song, and has thus rendered
old Scotia ever dear to all mankind. If the
human heart ever turns with a passionate
longing to our own southland, it will not be in
quest of traditions of their great warriors and
statesmen, but rather to revel in the songs, the
sorrows, the sighings, and the spiritual striv-
ings as embodied in the plantation melodies.
Which of her patriotic odes would America not
willingly give away in exchange for "Swing
low, sweet chariot," or "Steal away to Jesus?"
Or where can be found a pathetic or patriotic
appeal more racy of the soil and melting to the
soul than "Way down upon the Suwanee
River"? It is curious that the negro furnished
the musical inspiration for the Southern Con-
federacy, for the famous song of *Dixie* merely
expresses the longing of the slave to return to
his native home "way down South in Dixie."
It is claimed that this is a white man's country. This proposition is understandable when
we consider that the white race constitutes
eight-ninths of its population, and has absorbed a still larger proportion of its material
and substantial strength; and, representing as
they do the most populous and powerful factor,
they are fairly entitled to, as they are in the
habit of securing, all that justly belongs to

them: but, according to any just and righteous standard, this country belongs to the negro as much as to any other, not only because he has helped to redeem it from the wilderness by the energy of his own arm, but because he has also bathed it with his blood and watered it with his tears, and hallowed it with the yearning of his soul.

Not only in local attachment, but also in devotion of spirit to American institutions and ideals, the negro has played a notable part. It was the negro slaves whose blood was first shed in the streets of Boston as an earnest of American independence. The statue of Crispus Attucks on Boston Common was doubtless intended to typify the spirit of the revolutionary war, but it has a deeper and muter meaning. It illustrates the self-sacrificing patriotism of a transplanted race. In every national crisis the negro has demonstrated his patriotism anew. It runs like a thread through every chapter of our national history from Boston Common to San Juan Hill. His soldierly service has not been that of the Hessian hireling peddling his prowess for pay, or the cowardly conscript forced to the front by the bayonet behind, but he has ever rushed to his country's battle line with his country's battle cry exultant on his lips. He was with Washington in the days of Valley Forge. He was with Jackson behind the fleecy breastwork of New Orleans. He responded two hundred thousand strong to the call of Father Abraham for the preservation of this Union; and it was his valor, as much as any other, that placed the American standards on the Spanish ramparts in the West Indies. Is it a political as it is a sacred principle that without the shedding of blood there is no remission of sins? If this be true, when we consider the blood of the captive making red the Atlantic current on his way to cruel bondage, the blood of a slave drawn by the lash, the blood of a soldier shed in behalf of his country, the blood of the victim of cruelty and outrage, we may exclaim, with Kipling:

> "If blood be the price of liberty,
> If blood be the price of liberty,
> If blood be the price of liberty,
> Lord God! he has paid in full."

It does seem remarkable that this crude, untutored race, without the inheritance of freedom, should display such an absorbing passion for free institutions. Throughout the whole range of sectional contention the negro has been on the side of liberty, law and national authority. On the whole he has advocated the party,

men, measures and policies that were calculated
to uphold the best traditions and the highest
American ideals. He is passionately attached
to party organization, which embodies principles too subtle to be grasped in the abstract.
His attachment to the party of Lincoln and
Sumner was characterized by blind hysteria
verging on fanaticism. He did not regard it as
an instrument to be used, but as a fetish to be
worshiped. He bowed down before it with
reverence and gratitude and awe, as Friday
before the gun of Robinson Crusoe because it
had once rescued him from circumstances of
great peril. This is the manner in which the
negro manifested patriotism. To him party
signified all that there was noble and worthy
in the country. All else was ruin and destruction. His ablest and most sagacious leader,
Frederick Douglass, at that time counseled
that the "Republican party is the ship; all else
is the sea." The verdict of history will show
that even this excessive party devotion was
in the line of the highest and best patriotism,
for the party of his love was, at that time, the
exclusive party of progress and freedom. The
political historian will seek in vain to find in
any national or local crises that the negro has
ever upheld unworthy local or national aim or
ideal. The possibility of such patriotic devo-

tion ought to convince the nation that the black race is a natural storehouse of loyalty which it may yet be called upon to utilize in the day of peril. No people of Anglo-Saxon breed would, like the negro, practice civic and political self-sacrifice, and say to their country, "Though you slay me, yet will I serve you."

By what possible stretch of argument can a race with such potential patriotic capacity be construed into a menace to free institutions? If there be any menaceful feature in the negro's political status, it is merely that he grows out of poverty, ignorance and the resultant degradation. These are only temporary and incidental, and they endure only until adequate means are put forward for their removal. There are some who are blinded by the spirit of racial animosity and hate, and with whom racial passion is the only political stock-in-trade, so that they will willingly create a racial menace where none exists, or perpetuate it though it might easily be removed. These are the most unloyal, unpatriotic men in America, and could profitably sit at the feet of the negro, whom they hold in despite, and learn the fundamental principles of loyalty and devotion to country and its cause.

That the negro is unfit to participate in any

degree in the affairs of government passes as a political axiom in some sections of the country. Whoever dares question the validity of this axiom by that action puts himself outside the pale of tolerant consideration. Acquiescence is the one test of political and social sanity. Men always resent the attempt to uproot their fondly cherished dogmas, especially if they inure to their benefit or appeal to their vanity; but, like most passionate dogmas, this one fails of substantiation when subjected to practical test. Its only support is a vehement and intolerable spirit which is appealed to as the first and last principles of argument. Experience does not show that, where the negro exercises the untrammeled right of franchise, he ever votes for men or measures inimical to the best welfare of the country at large or of the community in which he resides. In Missouri, Kentucky, West Virginia, and Maryland, where the negro vote represents a considerable fraction of the total electorate, negro voters uniformly support the best men and measures put forward in their respective States. The men who, in these border States, have succeeded to office largely on the basis of negro votes stand, and have always stood, for the best local and national ideals. If we take the personnel of the Senators, Representatives, and local officials with negro support, and compare them with the corresponding officials, on the basis of an exclusive white electorate, the former would suffer no whit by comparison either in ability, devotion or patriotic integrity. In a border State, where the negro vote constitutes one-fifth of the total electorate, desperate efforts have been made to eliminate him from the franchise. The reasons urged are mainly speculative and frenzied. The most ardent eliminationist may be confidently challenged to point out where the negro vote in that State has ever resulted in the choice of unworthy or incompetent public servants, or has promoted measures contrary to the peace, progress and well being of the commonwealth. Since reconstruction, numerous negroes have filled official positions under the government, both elective and appointive. They have usually conducted the business committed to them to the entire satisfaction of the people, and have been subjected to the same test of competency as white officials in like situations. The chief federal official in a Southern State is a negro who has filled the position for thirteen years, and holds a record of efficiency comparable with any official of his grade in the entire public service. Protest against such officials is not because they are incompetent or undeserving, but merely because, for racial reasons, they are considered undesirable. If the reasoning might be put in a logical formula, it would run thus: "The white man should rule: therefore, the negro is unfit to exercise any of the functions of government." Or, as a famous critic once said, "Shakespeare should not have painted Othello black, because a hero of a drama ought to be white."

The negro is now passing through the most distressing stage of his political experience. He stands listlessly by as his political rights are denied, his privileges curtailed, and the current of public feeling grows cold and chilly. The constitutional amendments in the reconstruction states have been and are inspired by the purpose to eliminate the black factor from the governmental equation. This is the overt or covert intention of them all. By the utmost stretch of ingenuity and strain of conscience the technical phrasing of the letter may seem to square with constitutional requirements, but there is no room to doubt the underlying spirit and purpose. It does not lessen the fraudulent quality of fraud by giving it legal sanction. These tricky and ingenious instruments may seem to do credit to the cunning of their devisers, but they portray a lamentable state of the conscience. If the offence must needs come, it were far better that the wrongdoer should sin against the law than that the seared conscience of the State should enact an unrighteous code. President Taft has explained, in extenuation of the devious devices to eliminate the negro, that statesmen in the individual States growing weary of individual fraud and violence preferred that the State should relieve the individual conscience by a legal sanction. We condemn butchery and slaughter in Turkey, not because they are more outrageous than the innumerable murders and lynchings in the United States, but because they have the tacit or avowed sanction of constituted authority. Lynching is the outbreak of an evil propensity which constituted authorities are either unable or unwilling to check; but is it not infinitely better that, if lynchings must needs be, they should stand as an expression of individual sin against the law rather than that they should be sanctioned by law?

No law, whether enacted by God or man, has ever been perfectly obeyed. The Ten Commandments have been violated hourly ever since they were announced amid the thunder and smoke of Mount Sinai. Should the Divine Author, therefore, modify his law to accommodate human frailties and imperfections? Above all things the organic laws of a State should be fair and candid, and should recommend themselves to the conscientious approval of all honest and upright citizens. Great indeed is the condemnation of that commonwealth whose organic law rests upon the basis of a lie.

These disfranchisement measures, harsh and severe as they are in many features, meet with little or no opposition from the nation at large. Although the clear and unmistakable intent of the Federal Constitution is set at naught, yet the nation suffereth it to be so. There is no moral force in the nation at present that will lead to their undoing, and no political exigency seems to demand it. That they violate the spirit, if not the letter, of the Federal Constitution is notorious. Every fourteen year old child in America is fully aware of this fact, and yet the nation winks at the violation of its own fundamental law. Men of the highest patriotic and personal probity ignore their oath to execute the law, and condone its annulment. If there is a growing disrespect for law in the attitude of the American mind, the cause is not far to seek nor hard to find. If one portion of the organic law may be violated with impunity, why not another if it seems to conflict with our interests or with our prejudices?

The negro is impotent. He makes his puny

protest, but the nation heeds it not. It is like
sheep proclaiming the law of righteousness to
a congregation of wolves. A complaint is effective only in so far as there is power to enforce it. That individual, race or nation is
considered cowardly, and justly so, that will
not use all available means to enforce a proper
recognition of its rights and prerogatives;
while the world looks with contempt upon a
people who allow themselves to suffer wrong
and injustice without using the most effective
protests at their command. It also despises a
lachrymose race which possesses no language
but a cry. The sufferer owes it to the wrongdoer, not less than to himself, not to remain
impassive or indifferent under outrage or
wrong. It lowers the moral status of the
perpetrator, not less than the victim, to encourage him to continue in his career of evil-
doing with none to molest or make afraid.

The Anglo-Saxon race boasts that it neither
needs nor heeds a law in face of its imperial
will. It is his imperturbable spirit

> That bids him flout the laws he makes,
> That bids him make the laws he flouts.

And yet this imperturbable race must be
amenable to the ethic principles which operate
regardless of ethnic proclivities. The ques-

tion as to whether might makes right must be relegated to the realm of pure morals; but sensible men know that might is still the effective force in practical government. In spite of constitutional compacts or written pledges, the strong will rule the weak, the rich will control the poor, and the wise will dominate the simple. In such contingencies we can always foretell the outcome with the predictive decision of natural law, and we may rely upon the prediction with the same assurance as we expect sparks to fly upward, or water to seek its level. This may not be the written law nor the preached gospel, but in its effective sanction of the practical conduct of men it is stronger than either. Social forces work out their inevitable results as assuredly as natural causes. The laws of social evolution are not going to suspend their operation. No one expects that the earth will again stand and gaze like Joshua's moon on Ajalon until a feebler contestant wins a victory over a more powerful adversary. If history teaches any clear lesson it is to the effect that the developed races are superior in all practical tests of power to the backward ones. This is especially true in the political arena. It is in this sphere that the Anglo-Saxon race manifests its peculiar genius. World-wide dominion seems to be in

the line of its natural destiny. The Englishman has clearly manifested his political superiority over the Asiatic as did the old Ro-
man over the Gaul and Briton. A handful of
Englishmen control the destiny of two hundred
million dusky Hindoos with as much ease as
the legions of Cæsar controlled the nomads of
the forests of northern Europe. This political dominance is not due to an attribute of
blood, but rises from a practical efficiency
gained through the discipline of civilization.
Thirty thousand American co-Liberians are
able to keep under governmental control two
millions of native Africans by reason of their
superior discipline and efficiency; all of which
goes to show that it is not blood but circumstances and conditions that count for political
dominance. Negro domination is an absurd
and impossible issue which has served only
sinister political ends. The negro, with his traditional handicaps and political ineptitude, can
no more dominate any section of the nation
than the babies in the cradle. But conscience
makes political cowards who tremble at a
shadow. A timid statesmanship is dominated
by a fancied dread which sober judgment
shows to be impossible of realization.

The question of government of a heterogeneous population is always one of great diffi-

culty and complexity. The racial situation in
the United States leads to an endless tangle.
The negro is promiscuously scattered throughout the entire white population. The unequal
density of distribution complicates the political
question. If there were territorial compact-
ness of this racial element, or if it were equally
diffused throughout the whole area, the problem in its political aspect would be greatly sim-
plified. It is a much simpler problem to formulate a satisfactory plan of political privilege
for the Philippine Islands than it is for South
Carolina or Alabama. The Filipino has territorial and racial solidarity, whereas in the
South two dissimilar classes cover the same
area. It is always easier to govern one race
than two. On the other hand, if the negro were
equally distributed among the States he would
not constitute more than one-eighth of the
strength of any community, and there would
scarcely be any necessity for special political
plans or policies to cover his case. As a political factor he would be absorbed in the general
equation. The very complexity of the racial
situation will ultimately compel political and
civil uniformity. In this country political, social and economic conditions gravitate toward
equality. We may continue to expect thunder-
storms in the political firmament so long as

there exists inequality of political temperature in the atmosphere of the two regions. Neither Massachusetts nor Mississippi will rest satisfied until there is an equality of political condition in both States. We are just beginning to appreciate the full significance of Abraham Lincoln's philosophy when he said that this country cannot exist "half slave and half free." Democratic institutions can no more tolerate a double political status than two standards of ethics or discrepant units of weight and measure.

All patriotic citizens must be interested in any honest effort to purify and elevate the suffrage. Honest effort to eliminate ignorance and corruption, in order to promote good government for all the people, must be appreciated as a political exigency, if not approved as a political principle. But no plan, not based on racial grounds and operated by tricky and fraudulent manipulation, can be devised which will shut in all white men and shut out all negroes. No such racial separatrix can be found. The clear purpose of the revised constitution, as is shown by ancestor clauses as well as by unfair manipulation of these laws between the races, is to eliminate the negro wholly from all governmental control. The negro is willing to take any test which the white race is willing to

impose upon itself. He is willing to drink of
the political cup of which the white man drinks,
and to be baptized with the baptism with which
he is baptized withal.

There are in the United States ten millions
of negroes, a large proportion of whom possess the requisite intelligence and general qual-
ification for the exercise of the high function
of citizenship, and yet they are without a voice
in the government. There is no negro in either
House of the National Congress, scarcely one
in any State Legislature, to make the laws by
which the race is to be governed, nor yet a
judge on the bench to interpret these laws, nor
an administrative officer to enforce them. If
the nation desires the negro to develop into
an effective factor of the American people he
must be given the same consideration, both before the law and behind the law, as enjoyed by
his white fellow-citizens. He merely asks for
equality of rights; no more, no less, no other.

The contention that in a heterogeneous racial situation one race alone must govern is
without sanction either in ethics or experience.
No man is good enough to govern another without his consent. The rich are not good enough
to govern the poor; the Protestant is not good
enough to govern the Catholic; the white man
is not good enough to govern the negro. The

class that is shut out from all participation in government will soon be shut out from participation in everything else that is worth while and that the controlling class covets. The privilege to work, to acquire an education, and to accumulate property is indeed of great value, but it cannot atone for the loss of the right to vote, which under our scheme of government is the right preservative of all other rights and privileges.

Experience shows that schemes of disfranchisement are always accompanied by vehement onslaught on the negro, and proscriptive legislation restricting his general welfare. It is noticeable that, in sections of cities where disfranchised negroes reside, there are few public improvements, because the residents have no voice directly or indirectly in the choice of the city councilmen. The black resident has no say as to who shall be alderman from his ward, and consequently this prudent official, exercising ordinary political sagacity, gives first consideration to the insistent claims of his white constituents, who can influence his continuation in office. It is a law of human nature that where we are intent on our own interests we abate our zeal for the welfare of others who may not be insistent upon their own claims. If the Protestants had exclusive

control of government, the Catholics would
have little show of a "square deal" where
their interests seemed divergent from or in conflict with the welfare of the dominant creed. It
is precisely for this reason that all elements in
a heterogeneous population should have some
say in the common government. This country
is making a mistake by depriving the negro of
all participation in government, locally and na-
tionally. The negro should be taught the beneficent purpose and principles of law and
order. He should be led to have implicit faith
in the righteousness and integrity of the law.
Good citizenship cannot be secured by holding
up the harsh, the cruel and repressive features
of government. The policeman's club is often-
times the only governmental instrument with
which the negro comes in contact. No other
enlightened nation on earth adopts this method
of dealing with a backward or retarded people.
England, France and Germany always make
such a people see and appreciate the beneficent
ends of government by making them a participant factor in it. There is no enlightened
government on earth, with a prudent regard
for its own best interests, that ruthlessly over-
rides the sensibilities of the governed.

The political status of the negro will probably culminate under the administration of

President Taft.[1] If by tacit acquiescence he lends implied encouragement to the retrograde tendencies of the times, the repeal of the Fourteenth and Fifteenth Amendments, which is now merely a matter of academic discussion, may become a practical issue. If on the other hand the last two amendments of the Constitution are regarded as a vital part of that instrument whose enforcement is regarded in the obligation of his high office, then an affirmative attitude will do much to check the growing sentiment which makes the last addition to the highest law of the land void and of no effect. President Taft comes of the highest patriotic and philanthropic ideals and traditions; but the tangle of the race problem will not yield to a generous disposition and personal goodwill, of which the President has an unlimited endowment. To the negro the danger seems that he may allow the rights of the race to be sacrificed on the altar of other pressing national problems. His ardent desire to establish peace and goodwill between the North and the white South must meet with sympathetic response in the heart of every true and loyal American; but a sacrifice of the Fourteenth and Fifteenth Amendments is too great price

[1] This essay was written during the early part of President Taft's administration.

to be paid even for a consummation so devoutly
to be wished. Mr. Taft is the first American
President to come to the office with a colonial
experience and policy whose very foundation
rests upon the inferior political status of the
subject race. It is easy to transfer the habit
of mind and bias of feeling from the Filipino
in the islands to the negro in the States. In
his letter of acceptance Candidate Taft said
that he stood unequivocally by the Fourteenth
and Fifteenth Amendments of the Constitution,
both in letter and spirit. His advisory, though
unofficial, attitude in the recent campaign in
Maryland was to the same effect. But these
utterances were more than offset by the statement in his inaugural address to the effect that
he would not appoint colored men to office
where local opposition was gathered. This suggestion is sufficient to invite the fiercest antagonism to the appointment of a negro to a Federal office in any community in the United
States. It seems somewhat anomalous that in
some places, where the majority of the population are negroes who belong to the President's
political party, no one of this race can be appointed to any Federal office if the minority,
who opposed his election, should enter protest.
From the present appearance of things, under
the operation of the announced policy of the

President, there will probably not be a negro officeholder in the South by the close of his administration. The elimination of the negro from office in the South means his eventual elimination in the nation. Elimination from office means elimination from politics.

The fact that a Cabinet officer, in open public utterances, boldly advocates the elimination of the negro from politics gives the whole race much anxiety. Usually a Cabinet Minister voices the policy and purpose of the administration of which he forms a part. President Taft has finished the first year of his administration. His policies are not yet distinctive and definitely set. It does not yet clearly appear what they shall be. Every patriotic and loyal citizen should be patient with an administration charged with such heavy duties and responsibilities, even though it may not be able at once to stress the issues in which he is especially, even vitally, concerned. The negro is watching the administration of President Taft with hopes and fears. May his hopes be triumphant over his fears.

FIFTY YEARS OF NEGRO EDUCATION

Experience is the rational outcome of experiment. Where there are neither fixed principles nor established precedent, the practical worker must feel after the right way, if haply he might find it. But he must have an open mind, ready to accept proved and tested results, and to discard discredited processes undertaken as an experimental necessity with equal acquiescence and cheerfulness of spirit.

Previous to the Civil War scattered schools for the instruction of persons of color existed in the North, and, to some extent, in a few Southern cities as well. Here and there a pious master or kindly mistress would teach a favorite slave the rudiments of knowledge, with connivance, evasion, or defiance of forbidding laws. Now and then an ambitious minded slave would snatch furtive bits of knowledge, with the traditional relish of stolen waters.

But, broadly speaking, it might be said that fifty years ago the systematic education of the negro race began near the absolute zero point of ignorance. The real intellectual awakening of the race began with the overthrow of slavery. When the smoke of war had blown away, when the cessation of strife proclaimed the end of the great American conflict, when the "war drum throbbed no longer, and the battle flags were furled," there emerged from the wreck and ruin of war 4,000,000 of human chattels, who were transformed, as if by magic, in a moment, in the twinkling of an eye, from slavery to freedom, from bondage to liberty, from death unto life. These people were absolutely ignorant and destitute. They had not tasted of the tree of knowledge which is the tree of good and evil. This tree was guarded by the flaming swords of wrath, kept keen and bright by the avarice and cupidity of the master class. No enlightened tongue had explained to them the deep and moral purpose of the Ten Commandments and the Sermon on the Mount. They were blind alike as to the intellectual and moral principles of life. Ignorance, poverty, and vice, the trinity of human wretchedness, brooded over this degraded mass and made it pregnant. The world looked and wondered. What is to be the destiny of this people? Happily, at this tragic juncture of affairs, they were touched with the magic wand of education. The formless mass assumed symmetry and shape. Nowhere in the whole sweep of history has the transforming effect of intelligence had a higher test of its power.

The circumstances amid which this work had its inception read like the swift-changing scenes of a mighty drama. The armies of the North are in sight of victory. Lincoln issues his immortal Emancipation Proclamation; Sherman, with consummate military skill, destroys the Confederate base of supplies, and marches through Georgia, triumphant to the sea; Grant is on his road to Richmond; the Confederate capital has fallen; Lee has surrendered; the whole North joins in one concerted chorus: "Mine eyes have seen the glory of the coming of the Lord." These thrilling episodes will stir our patriotic emotions to the latest generations. But in the track of the Northern army there followed a band of heroes to do battle in a worthier cause. Theirs was no carnal warfare. They did not battle against flesh and blood, but against the powers of darkness intrenched in the minds of an ignorant and degraded people. A worthier band has never furnished theme or song for sage or bard. These noble women—for these people were mostly of the female sex—left homes, their friends, their social ties, and all that they held dear, to go to the far South to labor among the recently emancipated slaves. Their courage, their self-sacrificing devotion, sincerity of purpose and purity of motive, and their unshaken faith in God were passkeys to the hearts of those for whom they came to labor. They were sustained by an unbounded enthusiasm and zeal amounting almost to fanaticism. No mercenary or sordid motive attaches to their fair names. They gave the highest proof that the nineteenth century, at least, has afforded that Christianity has not yet degenerated to a dead formula and barren intellectualism, but that it is a living, vital power. Their works do follow them. What colored man is there in all this land who has not felt the uplifting effect of their labors? Their monument is builded in the hopes of a race struggling upward from ignorance to enlightenment, from corruption to purity of life. These are they who sowed the seeds of intelligence in the soil of ignorance and planted the rose of virtue in the garden of dishonor and shame. They had no foregoers; they have no successors. It is said that gratitude is the fairest flower that sheds its perfume in the human heart. As long as the human heart beats in grateful response to benefits received, these women shall not want a monument of living ebony and bronze.

Those who enlisted in this cause had neither the lamp of experience to guide their feet, nor yet the assurance of hoped for results to strengthen their faith. At that time not only the policy, but the possibility, of educating the negro was in the bonds of dialectic doubt and denial. It was the generally accepted dogma of that day that the negro was not amenable to the intellectual and moral régime applicable to the white child. The institution of slavery made requisition upon the negro physical faculties alone, and therefore the higher susceptibilities of his nature were ingeniously denied and prudently suppressed. Ordained intellectual and moral inferiority is the only valid justification of political and social subordination. Hence, this became the ultimate dogma of the pro-slavery propaganda. Those who profess to doubt the possibilities of human nature are never quite sure of the foundation of their belief. Although the loud boast is ever on their lip, their conduct reveals the secret suspicion of the heart for fear it might be so. Thus we see that those who most confidently proclaim that the negro, by nature, is incapable of comprehending the intellectual basis of the Aryan culture and civilization are ever on the alert to prevent him from attempting the impossible. If the negro's skull was too thick to learn, as the dogma ran, why pass laws forbidding him to try? But after all it must be said that the slave régime possessed the wisdom of its policy and practiced the cunning necessary to carrying it out. It was deemed dangerous to communicate to the despised negro the mystic symbols of knowledge which reveal all the hidden secrets of civilization. This policy was based upon the well-founded fear of primitive jealousy: "Lest he should stretch forth his hand, and partake of the tree of knowledge, and become as one of us." But the flaming sword of jealousy and wrath can not for long guard the tree of knowledge against the quest of those who would partake of the fruit thereof. No one who sniffs the ozone of an atmosphere surcharged with the doctrine of equality, and to whom has been vouchsafed the talisman of knowledge, will ever be satisfied with a status that assigns him to a rank below the level of his faculties. Under the ancient régime of acknowledged and accepted political and social subordination, masters took pride in educating their apt and capable slaves. Indeed several names of this class attained the rank of respectable philosophers whose fame reaches down to our own day. But the doctrine of freedom and equality is a sure and

swift contagion, without respect of race or
color.

The missionaries who first came down from
the North were not generally educators according to the requirements of the modern education. They brought the technical terms of
knowledge in their left hand. In their right
hand they brought religion, culture, civilization. They quickened the spirit, aroused the
energies, and awakened the consciousness of a
suppressed race that had been so long despised
and rejected. As the traditional treatment had
rested upon professed disbelief in the negro's
capabilities, the method of the missionaries
was based upon the belief in higher human possibilities. The colder calculating spirit of this
later day may, with supercilious disdain, call
it fanatacism, but none can deny its uplifting
and sustaining power.

The missionary and religious organizations
vied with one another in planting institutions
of higher pretensions for the recently emancipated class. The establishment of institutions
on the higher level of European culture for a
people who had hitherto been denied the al-
phabet was a most daring experiment. It was
a severe test of the faith of the founders. But
fifty years of experience has abundantly justified the experiment. If we should subtract

from the development of the negro life the influence contributed by and attributable to these much berated negro colleges and universities, the remainder would be niggardly indeed.

Of late we have heard much criticism to the effect that education of the race began on top instead of at the bottom. Naturally enough, these schools were patterned after the traditional academic type then prevailing in New England. Indeed, the education of people should begin at the top, if we are to look to historical development of the human race for the proper method. In education, as in religion, the good things proceed from above, and trickle downward, carrying their beneficence to the masses below. Just as Yale and Harvard are the foster mothers of New England educational progress, so these negro universities and colleges produced the teachers, ministers, physicians, lawyers, editors and enlightened leaders who are guiding and directing the race life to-day along better ways.

The Freedmen's Bureau coöperated with the missionary and religious societies in promoting the education of the recently emancipated slaves. These coöperating agencies, governmental and private, were conducted by men of like mind and spirit as regards the needs of the field in which they were engaged. On the dissolution of the Bureau, many of its agents took leadership in the recently founded colleges and universities. Its chief officer, General O. O. Howard, became president of the principal school which the bureau had founded or fostered. When the reconstruction governments were organized in the Southern States they made provision for the public education of all children, black and white, as part of the organic law. These governments have been and are still held up to public obloquy and scorn by those whose ambition has been promoted by their overthrow. But they have to their everlasting credit this one unchallenged measure of statesmanship, which is not equaled in the legislative annals of either the old South or the new.

At the time of the founding of these schools industrial training was, nowhere in America, considered a stated part of the educational program. Indeed specific scholastic preparation for life's work was limited to the learned professions. A knowledge of the three R's was considered adequate preparation for the ordinary duties of life. Fifty years ago General C. S. Armstrong stood almost alone as the earnest advocate of industrial training as an agency for fitting the freedmen for their new function. To-day, the necessity for this manual training, not only for black boys, but for all of the sons and daughters of toil who must shortly join the ranks of the world's workers, is universally acknowledged and extolled. Occupational training will demand a larger and larger place in the educational program of the future.

With the rise of industrial schools there sprang up a fierce and bitter controversy between the promotion of the two contrasted types of education. The one-eyed advocates aligned themselves in battle array, and would not so much as heed a flag of truce. Indeed the race problem seems to afflict the mind as a virulent intoxicant. Men of sane and sober judgment on ordinary issues seem to lose all logical balance and composure on this problem. Where passion enters, reason takes flight. The war between the hand and the head went merrily on. The situation was full of risible and grotesque possibilities. The Greek grammar and rosewood piano in a dingy cabin even now provoke mirth. The industrial advocates by adroit acquiescence in the political subjugation of the race gained the sympathy and assistance of those whose invariable policy is to reduce the negro to the lowest possible terms. Industrial education became a byword. In the mind of one man it meant that the negro should be

taught only to know the relative distance between two rows of cotton or corn, and how to
deport himself with becoming behavior behind
the chair while his white lord and master sits
at meat; while, in the mind of another, it stood
for the awakening of the best powers and possibilities. To the white man of the South it may
have meant that the negro was to be made more
serviceable to him and more easily amenable to
his imperious will. To the white man of the
North it may have meant that the black man
was to be made a competent worker, equipped
with intelligence and skill such as are demanded
of Northern workmen. However variant may
have been the interpretations of the meaning
of industrial education, there was a general
agreement to discredit the higher culture of the
race. The industrial advocates made the more
effective popular appeal. Philanthropic con-
tributions were turned into their coffers. The
college and university seemed doomed to star-
vation. But fortunately a more sober and rational spirit now prevails. The erstwhile partisan zealots are beginning to see what a dispassionate judgment has always made plain.
A population of people ten million strong, with
all the varied capacities, aptitudes, opportunities and inclinations of human nature, stands in
need of every form and variety of education

that counts for progress. Industrial and higher education are complementary factors of the same product. They are both essential parts of the educational program, each in its proper place and proportion. Howard and Hampton, Fisk and Tuskegee are in no sense antithetic institutions, but supplementary co-workers in the same field. It is perfectly evident that no one school, nor any single type of schools, is adequate to the wide circle of racial needs.

There are some good people who are generally well disposed to the race, but who think that every negro, whatever his future calling is to be, should be taught a hand trade; that every negro school, whatever its grade and pretension, should have industrial work as a part of its curriculum. They are always looking for the apron as the traditional racial badge. It is true that the great bulk of the race must for all time that we can foresee earn their living by some form of manual work. Therefore the industrial training should have a large place in the educational program. Its importance cannot be overemphasized. But there is a higher field of service, on the plane of directive intelligence and professional skill. The negro teacher needs to know as much respecting the needs and necessities of the growing mind as does the white pedagog. The negro physician meets with every form of sickness and disease that human flesh is heir to. The negro preacher certainly confronts as grave moral and spiritual problems as ever devolved upon the sacerdotal office. The best welfare of any people will not be long safeguarded unless they raise up from their own ranks men who have power and preparation to state their case and defend their cause before the just judgment of mankind. The blind must be led; the leaders must have vision. Those who must stand in the high places of leadership and authority need all of the strengthening and sustaining power that the highest discipline and culture of the school can afford.

These warring factions are now beginning to open both eyes and to appreciate the value of binocular vision. Dr. Booker T. Washington, the chief apostle of industrial training, has accepted a place on the governing board of Howard University, the leading school for higher culture. Neither has surrendered, but both have struck hands on the high ground of mutuality and good will.

Among the most interesting features of negro education may be mentioned the rise of State colleges. The Federal Government appropriates, through the land grant and the

Morrill fund, a given amount for the encouragement of agricultural and mechanical training in each state. In those states whose constitutions provide for a scholastic separation of the races these funds are divided pro rata to the racial population. As a result every Southern state has an agricultural and mechanical college for the negro race. These schools are placed under negro faculties, and the federal allowance is supplemented by state appropriations, as a partial offset to larger sums devoted to state colleges for the white youth.

Another class of schools which deserve special notice are those institutions which fall wholly under negro support and control. Each of the leading negro denominations has a chain of schools and colleges fostered along the lines of its denominational policy. These schools furnish a most hopeful and interesting indication; for, in education as in physics, no body can for long maintain its stable equilibrium whose center of gravity falls outside of the basis of support. Many of the most forceful leaders of the race, especially in religious work, are the product of these schools. They are usually characterized by a marvelous optimism and virility of spirit.

The negro race is generally referred to as a unit, and its needs and circumstances as requir-

ing a uniform mode of treatment. On the
other hand, there is no other class of our population that is subject to so wide a diversity of
conditions. Unlike the Indian, he lacks territorial solidarity and homogeneous environment.
There are about three-quarters of a million
negroes in the Northern and Western States,
in which there is no scholastic separation of
races. The colored children attend school
along with their white fellow-pupils, and dis-
tribute themselves among the several grades
and departments of instruction according to
circumstances, aptitude and opportunity. They
have open to them all of the educational facilities and privileges of the most favored portions of the nation. They do not, however, as
a rule, take advantage of these opportunities,
especially in the higher reaches of knowledge,
because they do not feel the keen incentive of
remunerative opportunity. It is only the boy
of exceptional ambition who will take the pains
to acquire an education which is not likely to
be called into requisition in the vocation which
he expects to follow. The occupational proscription of the North chills the ambition of
the negro youth, despite the allurements of
fine educational facilities. Several hundred
negro students are pursuing higher academic
and professional courses in Northern colleges

and universities. But, for the most part, they are from the South with the fresh inspiration of the masses upon them. The best schools in the country, both as regards public systems and chartered institutions, are open to all applicants who are able to meet the intellectual, moral and financial requirements. The scholastic separation of the races is only a local provision for states where the negroes are relatively numerous. Through the broad policy of the North and West, where our educational systems have the highest perfection, the negro is brought in touch with the best scholastic opportunities that the teaching world affords.

Again the educational needs of the city negro must be carefully differentiated from those of the rural masses. The general environment and practical conditions are so diverse that we must separate the two in any scheme of profitable discussion. There are about one and a half million negroes in Southern cities of 2,500 or more inhabitants. Adding these to the Northern fragment it leaves something like three-fourths of the race in the rural parts of the South.

In the cities school funds are quite sufficient to maintain the graded schools for the average length of term with the requisite facilities and appliances of instruction. The duplication of

schools for the two races works less economic
disadvantage in cities where the number of
both races is sufficient to supply adequate
school constituencies than in the country, where
the population is sparsely scattered. The education of the city negro makes little or no
claims on outside philanthropy. The cities are
well able to educate their own children, and
there is no more reason why they should seek
outside aid for this purpose than for any other
branch of municipal government. School teaching furnishes about the only avenue of remunerative employment for colored women
above the grade of domestic service, and hence
the best equipped members of the race rush
into this field of work. Negro school teachers,
male and female, are often the best paid wage-
earners in the several communities, and are
looked up to as leaders in social life and general
activities. This gives the negro schools a relative advantage which the whites do not enjoy.
The best equipped members of the white race
are usually engaged in more remunerative and
attractive pursuits. Such cities as Washington, Baltimore, St. Louis, Louisville and Little
Rock maintain high schools for colored youth
which do respectable secondary work, even
when measured by New England standards.
Even where the municipality does not make

provision for high schools, philanthropic and denominational institutions have made some provision, so that there is scarcely a city in the South of considerable negro population that has not a school of secondary pretensions, maintained at either public or private cost. Broadly speaking, educational facilities are open to urban negroes, which among white youth have been accounted sufficient to prepare for the ordinary duties of life. The pressing educational problem of the city negro is rather one of adaptation than enlargement. Education on its practical side should be shaped to the obtainable pursuits of the pupil. The peculiar situation and circumstances of the negro race adds new emphasis to several educational principles. The negro race furnishes the richest possible field for educational experiment. There is the broadest scope for originality, or at least the interpretation of general principles in terms of new conditions. The perfection of the urban schools is of higher importance to the welfare of the race at large, for it is in the city centers that the torch must be kindled that is to give light to the remotest rural ramifications.

The education of the country negro is of itself a thing apart. The means are so meager and the provisions are so inadequate that what little schooling he gets can be called education only by courtesy of speech. His life preparation is woefully inadequate to the requirements of intelligent citizenship. The demand is imperative that the Federal Government should bring the light of knowledge to the shady places of the South. Statesmanship and philanthropy might well unite upon this patriotic task.

The Peabody, Slater, Hand, Rockefeller and Jeanes Foundations have been devoted wholly or in part to the education of the Southern negro. But only the last named fund is aimed directly at the spot where the need is greatest.

Fifty years of negro education has accomplished certain definite results, and suggests certain definite needs.

In the first place, it has settled for all time the negro's capacity to comprehend the rudiments, as well as the higher reaches, of knowledge and apply them to the tasks of life. The race which was once denied the possession of an educationable mind is thus proved to be responsive to the same intellectual stimulus as the great Aryan race. Those who affect to doubt this proposition need themselves to be pitied for their evident incapacity to grasp demonstrated truth.

In the second place, the colleges and universities have furnished the teachers, preachers, doctors, lawyers, editors, and general leaders who are now directing the activities of the negro people, and stimulating them to higher and nobler modes of life. This professional class, like the priest Melchizedek, sprang at once to places of authority and leadership, without antecedents or beginning of days. The instrumentality which in some measure helped to fit them to their high function performed a service rarely, if ever, equaled in the history of human betterment.

In the third place, the illiteracy of the race has been cut down to forty-five per cent., which marks the most marvelous advance in the technical elements of knowledge in the annals of human progress. It is true that the vast majority of those classed as literate have a technical rather than a practical grasp of the principles of knowledge. Of those who *can* read and write, comparatively few *do* read and write effectively, and bring their acquisition to bear upon the common tasks of life. They do not generally pass constitutional tests in Alabama, as the knowing registration officers assure us. While it is true that a mere technical knowledge of letters may have little immediate bearing upon practical tasks, yet its potential value is beyond calculation. It is a possession that is not destroyed, but is carried forward. Literate parents transmit their acquisition to their children, so that the current of acquired knowledge flows on in an ever-deepening and widening channel. This mystic key with twenty-six notches unlocks all of the hidden secrets of the universe. It opens up newness of life. Transition of a people from illiteracy to literacy is like changing the temperature of a region from several degrees below to a few degrees above the freezing point. The actual change may seem to be small, yet it effects a marvelous transformation in the surrounding flora and fauna. And so with a race, the transmission of the symbols of knowledge acquired by a few years' schooling thaws out the faculties frozen by centuries of ignorance, which will shortly begin to yield a new flower and fruitage.

The cost of negro education for these fifty years has been a vast sum in the aggregate, but is utterly inadequate when counted against the task to which it has been applied. Northern philanthropy has contributed a princely sum, unequaled in any other domain of vicarious service. The Southern States have appropriated to this use a part of the public tax which the negro's industrial activities and economic position make possible. The asser-

tion that the Southern white man imposes a
gratuitous tax upon himself for the benefit of
the black man's education rests upon an economic fallacy and a total misapprehension of
the responsibility of the State to promote intelligent citizenship. The claim for equal educational facilities for the negro child is not based
upon civic charity, but upon justice and equity
and enlightened policy.

It is blatantly and bitterly asserted that
the education of the negro has not solved the
race problem. It was but a shallow philosophy
that prophesied this outcome in the first place.
Indeed much of the reversion of feeling against
the higher education was due to the fact that
after twenty-five years of effort the race problem had become rather intensified than abated
in acuteness. The industrial advocates shrewd-
ly enough promised the American people that
their program would result in the desired solution. The prophet always puts the fulfilment
as remote as possible from the prophecy and
relies upon popular forgetfulness to escape his
just condemnation. When the day of reckoning comes, as it surely must, those who promised to solve the problem through industrial
training will be declared to have been false
prophets. Education must not be condemned
as a failure because it has not accomplished

results that lie outside of the sphere of its function. All of our complex national problems are intensifying and growing apace with increase of education. Rapacity and greed, the tangle of labor and capital, the wrangle of rich and poor, municipal corruption, and crime against property and persons seem to proceed *pari passu* with increasing popular enlightenment. Shall we condemn the education of the American people because it does not settle these grave problems? In the North where the negro has educational advantages equal to those offered the most favored class of children anywhere on earth, and in the cities where fairly satisfactory provisions prevail, the race problem persists in its manifold forms and phases. Education enables the individual to grapple with his environment; it makes the race a component coöperating factor instead of a negative force in the general equations of progress. Without it the negro must hang as a millstone upon the neck of the nation's advance. For, in the nature of things, ignorance is a menace to knowledge, vice to virtue, and degradation to the decencies of life. But we misinterpret its function if we expect a few years' schooling to settle the problems growing out of the contact, attrition, and frictional relations of the races. These far-reaching questions depend upon a

larger policy, and must be left to statesmanship, philanthropy, and religion, and, most of
all, to the propitiation of time.

Fifty years' experience has also taught certain clear lessons as to method which should not
go unheeded.

Early educational effort in this field was devoted largely to building up religious adherents
within denominational lines. The negro race
has become attached to two leading denominations, from which there is not likely to be much
serious proselytism. As the Irishman is a
Catholic, the Scotchman a Presbyterian, so the
negro is a Baptist or a Methodist. It seems to
be a practical waste of time to attempt to wean
him from this adherence by educational induce-
ment. Up to a few years ago, Northern philanthropy was promoted largely by the religious
motive. But the denominational institutions
are becoming a diminishing factor in our general educational equation. They are not generally able to compete with those institutions
which appeal to all of the people without religious restriction. Since the organization of
the general Board of Education, this philanthropy seems to be prompted more and more
by a sense of civic and social service rather
than to promote any particular religious polity.
A wise coördination would obviate the waste

of needless duplication. There should be called
a conference of representatives of the various
religious organizations and other agencies, to
advise upon some comprehensive plan of artic-
ulation and coördination of work. There have
been founded more colleges and universities
than can be adequately maintained. The high
sounding pretensions of an institution above
the level of its grade and facilities tend to discredit the whole scheme in the minds of serious
and sensible men, and to give the negro youth
a false notion of what education really means.
This conference might well consider the advis-
ability of reducing the number of colleges to
five or six, distributed with reference to the
needs of the population, and of providing faculties and facilities that would enable them to
live up to the name assumed. The others might
well be limited to the secondary grade, as feed-
ers for the higher institutions or as finishing
schools of a lower order of pretension. The
proper distribution of industrial schools might
also claim the attention of this conference. Institutions maintained by private philanthropy
were at first compelled to assume the lowest
grades of instruction. But as the public
schools have developed this is no longer a
necessity. These institutions should relegate
to the public schools all work which falls within

their sphere, and confine their energies to those lines which fall beyond or at least outside of the scope of public instruction. It is needless to say that there should be the heartiest coöperation with Southern school authorities for the betterment of the public school system. Each Southern state should maintain a normal school, with facilities and equipment equal to the best requirements of the teaching world. The teacher is an agent of the state. It is as much a disgrace for a sovereign state to employ incompetent teachers to enlighten its future citizens as it would be to engage incompetent persons to conduct any other feature of its affairs.

If the experience of the past fifty years has done nothing but enable us to follow the right method in the future, the means and effort will not have been spent wholly in vain.

NEGROES IN PROFESSIONAL
PURSUITS

The world's workers may be divided into two well-defined classes: (1) Those who are concerned in the production and distribution of wealth, and (2) those whose function is to regulate the physical, intellectual, moral, spiritual and social life of the people. The sustaining element includes workers in the field of agriculture, domestic and personal service, trade and transportation, and in manufacturing and mechanical pursuits. The governing class comprises government officials, ministers, teachers, physicians, lawyers, editors and authors. The great bulk of the population representing the toiling masses is found under the first head, while a comparatively small number is required for the so-called learned professions. In the United States the two elements are divided in the approximate ratio of twenty to one. Traditionally these two classes have been separated by a wide and deep social gulf. All honor and glory have attached to the higher professional pursuits, while those who recruited the ranks of the toiling world have been accorded a distinctively lower order of consideration and esteem. The youth who were most highly gifted by nature or favored by fortune naturally sought careers in the genteel professions, leaving those of lesser gifts and limited opportunity to recruit the ranks of the lower order of service. The present tendency, however, is against this hard and fast demarcation. Distinction is made to depend upon success, and success upon efficiency, regardless of the nature of the pursuit or vocation. Honor and shame no longer attach to stated occupations or callings, but depend upon achievement in work rather than in choice of task.

The negro was introduced into this country for the purpose of performing manual and menial labor. It was thought that for all time to come he would be a satisfied hewer of wood and drawer of water and tiller of the soil. He was supposed to represent a lower order of creation, a little more than animal and a little less than human. The dominant dogma of that day denied him capacity or aspiration to rise above the lowest level of menial service. He was deemed destined to everlasting servility by divine decree. His place was fixed and his sphere defined in the cosmic scheme of things.

There was no more thought that he would or could ever aspire to the ranks of the learned professions than that a like ambition would actuate the lower animals. Much of this traditional bias is brought forward and reappears in the present-day attitude on the race problem. There still linger a rapidly diminishing element of infallible philosophers who assume intimate acquaintance with the decrees of the Almighty and loudly asseverate that the negro is God-ordained to everlasting inferiority. But those who assume foreknowledge with such self-satisfied assurance prudently enough fail to tell us of their secret means of familiarity with the divine plans and purposes. They do not represent the caliber of mind or quality of spirit through which such revelation is usually vouchsafed to man. From this school of opinion the negro's aspiration to enter the learned professions is met with ridicule and contempt. The time, money and effort spent upon the production and preparation of this class have been worse than wasted because they tend to subvert the ordained plan. Higher education is decried; industrial education, or rather the training of the hand, is advised, as the hand is considered the only instrument through which the black can fulfill his appointed mission.

But social forces, like natural laws, pay little

heed to the noisome declaration of preconceived opinion. The inherent capacities of human nature will assert themselves despite the denial of the doctrinaire. The advancement of the negro during the last fifty years has belied every prediction propounded by this doleful school of philosophy. Affirmed impossibilities have come to pass. The "never" of yesterday has become the actuality of to-day.

In a homogeneous society, where there is no racial cleavage, only the select members of the most favored class of society occupy the professional stations. The element representing the social status of the negro would furnish few members of the coveted callings. The element of race, however, complicates every feature of the social equation. In India we are told that the population is divided horizontally by caste and vertically by religion. But in America the race spirit serves as both a horizontal and vertical separation. The negro is segregated and shut in to himself in all social and semi-social relations of life. This isolation necessitates separate ministrative agencies from the lowest to the highest rungs of the ladder of service. During the days of slavery the interest of the master demanded that he should direct the general social and moral life of the slave. The sudden severance of this tie left the negro wholly without intimate guidance and direction. The ignorant must be enlightened, the sick must be healed, the poor must have the gospel preached to them, the wayward must be directed, the lowly must be uplifted, and the sorrowing must be solaced. The situation and circumstances under which the race found itself demanded that its ministers, teachers, physicians, lawyers, and editors should, for the most part, be men of their own blood and sympathies. The demands for a professional class were imperative. The needed service could not be effectively performed by those who assume and assert racial arrogance and hand down their benefactions as the cold crumbs that fall from the master's table. The help that is to be helpful to the lowly and the humble must come from the horizontal hand stretched out in fraternal good will, and not from the one that is pointed superciliously downward. The professional class who are to uplift and direct the lowly and humble must not say "So far shalt thou come but no farther," but rather "Where I am there ye shall be also."

There is no more pathetic chapter in the history of human struggle than the smothered and suppressed ambition of this race in its daring endeavor to meet the greatest social exigency to supply the professional demand of the

masses. There was the suddenness, the swift-
ness of leap as when a quantity in mathematics
changes signs, passing through zero or infinity.
In an instant, in a twinkling of an eye, the
plow-hand was transformed into the priest, the
barber into the bishop, the house-maid into the
school mistress, the porter into the physician,
and the day-laborer into the lawyer. These
high places of intellectual and moral authority
into which they found themselves thrust by
stress of social necessity had to be operated
with at least some semblance of conformity
with the standards which had been established
by the European through the traditions of the
ages. The high places in society occupied by
the choicest members of the white race after
years of preliminary preparation had to be assumed by men without personal or formal fitness. The stronger and more aggressive na-
tures pushed themselves to the higher callings
by sheer force of untutored energy and uncon-
trolled ambition. That there would be much
grotesqueness, mal-adjustment, and failure
goes without saying. But, after making full
allowance for human imperfections, the fifty
thousand negroes who now fill the professional
places among their race represent a remarkable body of men and indicate the potency and
promise of the race.

The Federal census of 1900 furnishes the latest available data of the number of negroes engaged in the several pursuits. Allowance, of course, must be made for growth in the several departments during the intervening thirteen years.

Negroes engaged in productive and distributive pursuits, 1900:

Agriculture	2,143,254
Domestic and Personal Service	1,317,859
Trade and Transportation	208,989
Manufacturing and Mechanical Pursuits	275,116
Total	3,945,118

Negroes engaged in professional service 1900:

Clergymen	15,528
Physicians and Surgeons	1,734
Dentists	212
Lawyers	728
Teachers	21,267
Musicians and Teachers of Music	3,915
Architects, Designers, Draughtsmen	52
Actors, Professional Showmen, etc	2,020
Artists and Teachers of Art	236
Electricians	185
Engineers and Surveyors	120
Journalists	210
Literary and Scientific Persons	99
Government Officials	645
Others in Professional Service	268
Total	47,219

From these tables it will be seen that only one negro worker in eighty-four is engaged in professional pursuits. Whereas, one white person in twenty is found in this class. According to this standard the negro has less than one-fourth of his professional quota.

The negro ministry was the first professional body to assume full control and direction of the moral and spiritual life of the masses. As soon as the black worshiper gained a conscious sense of self-respect, which the Christian religion is sure to impart, he became dissatisfied with the assigned seats in the Synagogue. The back pews and upper galleries did not seem compatible with the dignity of those who had been baptized into the fellowship and communion of the saints. With the encouragement of the whites the negroes soon set up their own separate houses of worship. There arose a priesthood, after the manner of Melchizedek, without antecedent or preparation. But notwithstanding all of their disabilities, these comparatively ignorant and untrained men have succeeded in organizing the entire negro race into definite religious bodies and denominational affiliations. The Baptist and Methodist denominations, which operate on the basis of ecclesiastical independence, have practically brought the entire race under their spiritual dominion. This is the one conspicuous achievement placed to the credit of the race by way of handling large interests. Passing over the inevitable imperfections in the development of the religious life of the race, the great outstanding fact remains that this vast religious estate comprising 30,000 church organizations, with a membership of over three and a half million communicants upon a property basis of $56,-000,000, has been organized and handed down as its most priceless inheritance. The negro church is not merely a religious institution, but comprises all of the complex features of the life of the people. It furnishes the only field in which the negro has shown initiative and executive energy on a large scale. There is no other way to reach the masses of the race with any beneficent ministrations except through the organizations that these churches have established. The statesmanship and philanthropy of the nation would do well to recognize this fact. The negro masses must be reached and uplifted through the instrumentality of the great Baptist and Methodist denominations, which alone can lay hold upon every man and woman of the race. Indeed, it is seriously to be questioned if any belated people, in the present status of the negro, can be wisely governed without the element of priestcraft. Broadly speaking, the negro is hardly governed at all by the State, but merely coerced and beaten into obedience. He is not encouraged to have any comprehensive understanding of or participating hand in the beneficent aims and objects of government. The sheriff and the trial judge are the only government officials with whom he is familiar; and he meets with these only when his life or his property is in jeopardy. If it were not for the church, especially the great Baptist and Methodist denominations, the great mass of the negro race would be wholly shut off from any organized influence touching them with any sympathetic intent. As imperfect as the negro church must be in many of its features, it is the most potential uplifting agency at work among the people. Eliminate the church and the masses of the people would speedily lapse into a state of moral and social degeneration worse than that from which they are slowly evolving. The great problem in the uplift of the race must be approached through the pulpit. The negro preacher is the spokesman and leader of the people. He derives his support from them and speaks, or ought to speak, with the power and authority of the masses. He will be the daysman and peacemaker between the races, and in his hands is the keeping of the destiny of the race. If these thirty thousand pulpits could be filled in this generation by the best intelligence, character and consecration within the race, all of its complex problems would be on a fair way to solution. The ignorance of the ministry of the passing generation was the kind of ignorance that God utilizes and winks at; but he will not excuse or wink at its continuance. It is a sad day for any race when the best they breed do not aspire to the highest and holiest as well as the most influential callings; but it will be sadder still for a retarded race if its ministry remains in the hands of those who are illy prepared to exercise its high functions.

The rise of the colored teacher is due to the outcome of the Civil War. The South soon hit upon the plan of the scholastic separation of the races and assigned colored teachers to colored schools as the best means of carrying out this policy. Hence, a large professional or semi-professional class was injected into the arena. There were at first a great many white teachers mainly from the North, but in time the task of enlightening the millions of negro children has devolved upon teachers of their own race. It was inevitable that many of the teachers for whom there was such a sudden demand should be poorly prepared for their work. It was and still is a travesty upon terms to speak of such work as many of them are able to render as professional service.

Among the white race the teacher has not gained the fullness of stature as a member of the learned professions. They do not constitute a self-directing body; both are controlled as a collateral branch of the State or city government, of which they constitute a subordinate part. The ranks are recruited mainly from the female sex. In case of the negro teacher these limitations are severely emphasized. The orders and directions come from the white superintendent, but there is some latitude of judgment and discretion in a wise and sensible adaptation. The great function of the negro teacher is found in the fact that she has committed to her the training of the mind, manners and method of the young, who are soon to take their place in the ranks of the citizenship of the nation. While there is wanting the independent scope which the preacher exercises in the domain of moral and spiritual control, nevertheless, the teacher exercises a most important function in the immediate matters committed to her. The negro teacher has the hardest and heaviest burden of any other element of the teaching profession. Education means more to the negro than it does to the white children, who from inheritance and environment gain a certain coefficiency of power aside from the technical acquisition of the schoolroom. The teacher of the negro child, on the other hand, must impart not only the letter, but also the fundamental meaning of the ways and methods of civilized life. She should have a preparation for work and a fixed consecration to duty commensurate with the imposed task.

The colored doctor has more recently entered the arena. At first the negro patient refused to put confidence in the physicians of his own race, notwithstanding the closer intimacy of social contact. It was only after he had demonstrated his competency to treat disease as skilfully as the white practitioner that he was able to win recognition among his own people. The colored physician is still in open competition with the white physican, who never refuses to treat the negro patient if allowed to assume the disdainful attitude of racial superiority. If the negro doctor did not secure practically as good results in treating disease as the white practitioner, he would soon find himself without patients. He must be subject to the same preliminary test of fitness for the profession and must maintain the same standard of efficiency and success. The negro physicians represent the only body of colored men who, in adequate numbers, measure up to the full scientific requirements of a learned profession.

By reason of the stratum which the negro occupies in our social scheme the race is an easy prey to diseases that affect the health of the whole nation. The germs of disease have no race prejudice. They do not even draw the line at social equality. The germ that afflicts the negro to-day will attack the white man to-morrow. One touch of disease makes the whole world kin, and also kind. The negro physician comes into immediate contact with the masses of the race. He is a sanitary missionary. His ministration is not only to his own race but to the community and nation as a whole. The dreaded white plague which the nation desires to stamp out by concerted action seems to prefer the black victim. The negro physician is one of the most efficient agencies in helping to stamp out this dread enemy of mankind.

The success of the physician has been little less than marvelous. In all parts of the country he is rendering efficient service and is achieving both financial and professional success. Educated negro men are crowding into this profession and will, of course, continue to do so until the demand has been fully supplied. The race can easily support twice the number of physicians now qualified to practice.

The negro lawyer has not been so fortunate as his medical confrère. The relation between attorney and client is not necessarily close and confidential as that of physician and patient, but is more businesslike and formal. The client's interests are also dependent upon the judge and jury with whom the white attorney is sometimes supposed to have greater weight and influence. For such reasons there are fewer negroes in the profession of law than in the other so-called learned professions. The negro lawyer is rapidly winning his way over the prejudice of both races just as the doctor has had to do. There are to be found in every community examples of the negro lawyer who has won recognition from both races, and who maintains a high standard of personal and professional success. A colored lawyer was appointed by President Taft as Assistant Attorney-General of the United States, and by universal testimony conducted the affairs of his office with the requisite efficiency and dignity.

As negro enterprises multiply and develop, such as banks, building associations and insurance companies, and the general prosperity of the people increases, the negro lawyer will find an increasing sphere of usefulness and influence.

Negroes are also found in all the list of professional pursuits and furnish a small quota to the list of editors, engineers, electricians, authors and artists. Merchants, bankers and business men are rapidly increasing in all parts of the country. Apprehension is sometimes felt that colored men will rush to the leading professions to the neglect of the humbler lines of service. The facts show that the race has not more than a fourth of its quota in the professional pursuits. The demand will always regulate the supply. When the demand has been supplied in any profession the overflow will seek outlet in unoccupied fields.

The uplift and quickening of the life of the race depend upon the professional classes. The early philanthropist in the Southern field acted wisely in developing leaders among the people. Philanthropy at best can only furnish the first aid and qualify leaders—they must do the rest. Any race is hopeless unless it develops its own leadership and direction. It is impossible to apply philanthropy to the masses except through the professional classes.

The higher education of the negro is justified in the requirements of the leaders of the people. It is a grave mistake to suppose that because he is relatively backward as compared to the white man, his leaders need not have the broadest and best education that our civilization affords. The more backward and ignorant the led, the more skilled and sagacious the leader should be. It requires more skill to lead the helpless than to guide those who need no direction. If the blind lead the blind, they will both fall into the ditch. The professional class constitutes the light of the race. The negro needs headlight to guide him safely and wisely amid the dangers and vicissitudes of an environing civilization. But if the light in that race be darkness, how great will be that darkness!

The negro teacher meets with every form of ignorance and pedagogical obtuseness that befalls the white teacher; the negro preacher has to do with every conceivable form of original and acquired sin; the doctor meets with all of the forms of disease that human flesh is heir to; the lawyer's sphere covers the whole gamut involving the rights of property and person. The problems involved in the contact, attrition and adjustment of the races involve issues which are intricate as any that have ever taxed human wisdom for solution. If, then, the white man who stands in the high places of authority and leadership among his race, fortified as he is by a superior social environment, needs to qualify for his high calling by thorough and sound educational training, surely the negro needs a no less thorough general education to qualify him to serve as philosopher, guide and friend to ten million unfortunate human beings.

"THE NEGRO IN THE NEW WORLD" *
AND "THE CONFLICT OF COLOR" †

These volumes represent bold and comprehensive attempts to grapple with the worldwide problems of race adjustment. The contact relation and final relations of the various races of mankind constitute the one all-embracing problem of modern civilization. The two volumes are devoted to the same general object, although the one is worldwide while the other is hemispheric in scope. Mr. Weale deals, in separate chapters, with the yellow, the brown and the black races in their relation to the European, while Sir Harry is concerned only with the African and the Caucasian in the New World. There are many points of agreement as well as striking divergencies. "The Negro in the New World" is the production of a scholar, with broad historical knowledge, long tropical residence and experience, wide observation, scientific spirit

* "The Negro in the New World," by Sir Harry H. Johnston.

† "The Conflict of Color," by B. R. Putnam Weale.

and philosophic turn of mind. On the other hand, "The Conflict of Color" is the attempt of an impatient publicist to promote a program with reliance upon race antipathy as the chief dynamic. The authors are alike unmitigated materialists and place as full and final reliance upon the concrete and practical factors of power in the final settlement of things as if they were dealing with the parallelogram of forces. They waive wide, as it were with the left hand, all restraint of conscience and higher sanctions of religion. Sir Harry ventures the judgment that the negro may in time rise to a position of "all around equality with the white man"; while Mr. Weale passionately espouses the age-worn dogma "that he cannot rise in the scale above a certain point." Both books lack the cohesiveness of consecutive and integral treatment due to the fact that the collected articles first appeared in scattered magazine form.

The "Negro in the New World" narrowly misses being a monumental treatise in the field traversed. In the wide range of historical, scientific and social knowledge, in firmness of grasp upon every essential feature of race relations during the last four centuries, it easily ranks among the first of books on the subject. The faults of the book are incident to the manner of its making. "The rolling stone gathers no moss" because its perpetual rolling does not give the spores the requisite time to take lodgment and reach structural maturity. And so the globe-trotting sociologist is not very apt to formulate a seasoned philosophy. Successive impressions are not given time to ripen into positive opinion or settled knowledge before others are superimposed, making a composite rather than a positive photograph. The sociological sojourner is always prone to hasty preachments, and is not willing to let his impressions convey their own lesson. The value of an impression is proportional to the object impressed; it may be made on mud or on marble. But the value and convincing power of a seasoned philosophy is independent of the medium by which it is conveyed. This book is a conglomerate of facts, historical and actual, impressions and preachments. The author also reaches general conclusions from insufficient induction. Single impressive incidents are magnified out of proportion to their inherent importance. For example, the author was so profoundly impressed with the work of Hampton and Tuskegee, involving some twenty-five hundred pupils, that he confined his treatment of negro education almost to these two foundations, with barely a word concerning the other negro universities and colleges with ten times as large a number or the great system of public schools with an enrollment of over a million.

The plan of the book is most excellent. The general conclusions are set forth in the preface, which are underpinned by subsequent chapters devoted to a detailed recital and analysis of history and actuality. There are several good maps and numerous excellent photographic illustrations. The first chapter is devoted to a labored effort to show that the negro belongs to a sub-species of the Genus Homo. The general reader will glance at the pictures as he flits the pages, but will pay little attention to finely and profoundly drawn ethnological analogies. However fascinating the discussion of the "os calcaneum" and the "plica semilunaris" may be to the scientific student, it makes the general reader somnolent.

The body and bulk of the book is devoted to a historical and present account of slavery under the several European powers, and the present position of the descendants of the African captives and their European captors in the West Indian archipelago, and in the two continents of the Western world. These chapters give the book its permanent importance and value. Indeed, if these chapters were disengaged from what precedes and follows and bound in a separate volume, the weight of its authority would be greatly enhanced.

His observations, impressions and conclusions concerning the present-day negro in the United States cannot be said to be in any marked way superior to those of several other writers, except that he shows throughout an inveterate hatred of cruelty and oppression, a genuine sympathy for the weak and overborne, and a fine sense of fair-play.

In "The Conflict of Color" Mr. Weale approaches the subject from the standpoint of an advocate defending a passionate dogma rather than a philosopher in quest of the truth. His general proposition is that the white race has been vouchsafed eternal dominion over the lesser breeds of men, yellow, black and brown, and that this dominion must be maintained though the heavens fall. With picturesque and characteristic portrayal he proclaims the imminent worldwide revolution, unless his program is followed. He holds a brief for the white race in general and for England in particular. In this threatened struggle between white men and non-white men "it is flesh and blood which form the true barrier." The dominant forces of the world are physiological and psychological. Of course, the innate everlasting superiority of the white man is assumed—

a superiority which, it is declared, exists even
after death. We read: ''The vigorous white
man even after death possesses a certain
majesty of form—a certain resolution—which
is totally lacking in the rice-fed Asiatics.''
Shakespeare tells us that ''Julius Cæsar dead
and turned to clay might stop a crack to turn
the wind away.'' Mr. Weale thinks that the
dust of the European is of finer quality than
that of other men. Separate chapters are devoted to the yellow, the brown and the black
factors of the problem. The final conclusion is
reached that the peace of the world depends
upon a nicely calculated balance of power
among the elements, the white man holding the
scales and England taking heed that the balance is true. Of course, the negro is accorded
the lowest position on the scale from which ''he
shall be lifted nevermore,'' according to Mr.
Weale's dismal philosophy. On this point the
author is wholly without originality. He
adopts the same hoary dogmas that have been
bandied about the world ever since the oldest
son of Noah took risible advantage of the bibu-
lous proclivities of that ancient patriarch.
''The black man is something apart—something untouchable.'' Along with received doc-
trines and animosities the author falls into the
traditional inconsistencies on this subject. The

anxiety to preserve race purity is a natural and
commendable one. "It is one of nature's most
zealously guarded laws"; this we read on page
230; five pages further on we note: "How to
keep races pure with his contact with them certainly is an acute problem; for, as he scatters
far and wide, he will leave—in spite of all pre-
cautions—some traces of his blood." The
writer must have forgotten his premises before
reaching his conclusion within the space of four
pages. What need is there of precaution to
enforce nature's "most zealously guarded
laws"? How is it that nature allows her laws
to be set aside even with the assistance, even
in spite of the vicarious assistance of precau-
tionary human prudence? A casual visit to
Rio de Janeiro, Brazil, or to Richmond, Virginia, would surely convince Mr. Weale that
for some centuries nature has been a great lag-
gard in enforcing her own zealously guarded
laws, and stands sorely in need of such assistance as his brand of statesmanship can afford.

Mr. Weale has also imbibed the traditional
intolerance of spirit. Such expressions as
"pulpit orators," "arm-chair philosophers,"
"ardent evangelists," and "individuals who
refuse to see things as they appear to the mass
of their countrymen and who simply argue
academically on all so-called color questions—

are not worthy of being read" sound quite
familiar to the student of anti-slavery and pro-
slavery literature. The real value of the book,
from a sociological point of view, consists in
the display and the interpretation of the statistics of the various races, the potentiality of
physical population, and the keen observation
that the momentum of racial flesh and blood
will probably fix the future bounds of habitation.

Taking these books together, which portray this great drama of which the world is the
stage, and the various races but players there-
on, one must feel that the vital weakness is
that they both, purposely and in set terms,
ruled out of account the motives which have
exercised the highest influence on human conduct throughout all history. It is indeed rather
fashionable in present-day philosophy to ignore religion as a practicable sociological factor.

Sir Harry avows that religious traditions
are not of the slightest practical utility in the
negro world of to-day. Mr. Weale declares
that religion has little to do with the standard
of living; religion has still less to do with the
balance of power; and it is these things alone
to-day which have a paramount racial importance. Again, avers Sir Harry: "Given the

same temptation and the same opportunities, there is sufficient of the devil left in the white man for the three hundred years of cruelty of negro (or other) slavery to be repeated, were it worth the white man's while." This is the severest indictment drawn against the claim of the Christian religion to assuage the inherent deviltry of man. The Christian conscience of this continent cannot allow this indictment to stand unchallenged. We need not be surprised, then, at Sir Harry's final statement: "Money solves all human difficulties. The one undoubted solution of the negro's difficulties throughout the world is for him to turn his strong arms, his sturdy legs, his fine sight, deft fingers, and rapidly developed brain to making money." The doctrine is of the earth earthy. The gospel, which is based upon the dollar as the highest common factor of values, cannot salve the deepest human feelings and passions. The dollar is mighty but not almighty. "The love of money is the root of all evil," says St. Paul, and subsequent history confirms the verdict. It is certainly the cause of the conflict of color throughout the world today. It was this "cursed love of gold" which brought the African to the Western World to exploit his physical capacities and which has carried Europeans to the ends of the earth seeking what lands and peoples they might devour.

Until there is developed a higher sanction, which transcends the physiological basis of flesh and blood, and the desideratum of the market place, there can never be peace and good will among the rival nations and races of men. To bring the world under the controlling sanction of science and religion, which ignores the prejudices and pretensions of the haughtier sections of the human race is "the one far-off divine event to which the whole creation moves."

THE MINISTRY

Is it not folly to encourage the "talented tenth" of the negro race when there is no outlet for its talent? The dollar is the highest common divisor of values, therefore all acquisition is useless which is not measured in terms of this standard. Of what avail is all of this vaporous effusion about knowledge and culture or the refinement of the higher faculties and finer feelings, if it cannot be reduced to a hard metallic basis according to the requirements of the market place? Why waste time in developing, on part of this despised race, susceptibilities which transcend things concrete and material? Can there be a more risible spectacle under heaven than a negro, whose income is less than that of a Pullman porter, reading Sophocles or descanting about Kant? If it be rejoined that Socrates in rags proclaimed the gospel of inner moral freedom; that Jesus redeemed the world without a bank account, and

that Robert Burns, in honest poverty, contributed an unrivaled share to the glory of his
beloved Scotia, such rejoinder is waived aside,
with the left hand, as being impertinent, or
sacrilegious. What has that sort of thing to
do with the benighted negro in Alabama? And
besides what does Wall Street care about such
impractical doctrinaires as Jesus, or Socrates,
or that scalawag of a songster, Robert Burns?
They are quoted by neither Bulls nor Bears,
and have no rating in Bradstreet's. We live
in a practical age, whose chief concern as re-
spects the negro is to make of him a more valuable material asset. Every able-bodied negro
ought to earn a dollar and a half a day—merely
this and nothing more. A higher compensa-
tion is likely to make him bumptious and for-
getful of his place. Away with your impotent
moralizers and dreaming doctrinaires. We
want something that is tangible, concrete and
constructive. We have a million dollars for a
workshop, but not one cent to encourage your
talented tenth who produce nothing but vac-
uous mouthings, inculcating false notions
among their people by holding out hopes impossible of realization. They are a plague to
both races.

Such is an interrogative or declarative interpretation of the prevalent attitude toward the

higher side of negro development. This attitude is in full consonance with the current philosophy of the times, which has little patience with ideals not quickly convertible into a cash equivalent. If Homer's Iliad were now originally appearing, it would doubtless be listed as the leading serial in one of the uplift magazines, and the public would be astounded to learn from red headlines that the author was offered a larger *per verba* honorarium than a noted explorer received for a description of his discovery of the North Pole, or the Intrepid One for an account of shooting wild beasts in the Jungle. What fabulous sum would not some enterprising journal offer for the exclusive copyright privileges on "The Sermon on the Mount," were it now proclaimed for the first time?

What more, then, need we expect from the conventionalized attitude toward a new people, just peeping above the horizon of the world's consideration, in such a time as this?

Ambition for Rulership

But, despite it all, the talented tenth of any people has an irrepressible ambition to assert and exert itself. The natural outlet for the energies of the upper ten is always in the higher domain of government, regulation and control of the lower ninety. What we shall eat or drink, or wherewithal we shall be clothed has never engaged the highest energies of the human mind. The functions of the talented tenth have always been devoted to the exercise of political, intellectual or spiritual leadership and authority over the masses. The regulative activities of society have always been conducted by a higher order of talent than the alimentary pursuits. Even where economic affairs seem to absorb a large proportion of the higher powers of the people, a closer scrutiny will disclose that the superior minds are devoted to leadership, guidance and control within the economic and industrial domain. This is the law of human evolution to which the negro forms no exception. A capable and enlightened leadership is the first prerequisite.

"For just experience proves in every soil
That those who think will govern those who toil."

THE CONTROLLING AGENCY

Political government is the controlling agency in society. The regulation of the religious and more intimate life of the people is relegated to the church whose sacred sanction is supreme within its sphere of operation. The secular and sacred phases of government are so nearly equal and parallel in their influence and power that we frequently observe that statecraft and priestcraft are united in a common control. The boast of America is that Church and State are separate and distinct institutions, each dominant within its own domain. But when we consider segregated elements of our population, like the Jew, the Catholic, and the negro, the sacred sanction is intensified in proportion as it is felt that the obligations and responsibilities of secular control are usurped or assumed by the large embracing body.

SELF-GOVERNMENT

All peoples, or segregated parts of peoples, desire self-direction and leadership. That governments derive their just powers from the consent of the governed passes, or used to pass, as a political axiom. That no people or class ever gives their unconstrained consent to have others rule over them is equally axiomatic. Whenever such a people are shut out from the general equation of the political government, they inevitably fall back upon the inalienable right of control over their own more intimate and social affairs. No wise ruler of a subject people ever attempts to interfere in the sacred sphere of such matters, so long as they keep within the established bounds of law and order. The negro is a subject class in the American body politic, and is' practically excluded from the political equation. Let us pass by, for the present, all ethical, or even prudential, considerations involved in this condition, and confine ourselves to the plain facts which are known and acknowledged of all men. This state of things is likely to continue as far into the immediate future as our powers of prevision can penetrate. In order that any class may form an effective part in governmental control it must not only possess the right of franchise, but must contribute to the personnel of the governing body. The right of suffrage is only political power in the passive voice; the active voice of government is vested in the officiary corps. No class of people may consider themselves an effective political factor unless a goodly number of the talented tenth may reasonably aspire to the pursuit of the Science and Art of government as a career. For the negro this is practically impossible. In the State of Georgia, where there are over one million negroes, constituting almost one-half of the population, there are 1,527 government officials; of this number only 54 are colored. It is well known that these are mostly in minor clerical positions under the federal authority, and that the number is likely to diminish rather than to increase. There is probably not a single negro in governmental place under state, county or municipal control. Out of 1,500 careers required for the government of this commonwealth, not a single one is open to the ambitious negro youth. It may be safely assumed that only those who find a livelihood in any pursuit are likely to follow that calling as a career. Elimination from office means elimination from politics. No negro can hope-fully aspire to be a Senator, Congressman, legislator, judge, diplomat, an officer in the Army or Navy, or even to hold important ap-pointive administrative positions. He is al-most as completely blocked from the game of politics as the female sex. Rash indeed would be considered that counsellor who should ad-vise an ambitious negro youth to engage in politics as a vocation.

The Field

Assuming then his inherent desire for self-leadership, and that the more highly endowed youth of this blood seek to exploit their powers in the direction, regulation and control of their fellowmen, where is the field to be found? Evi-

dently within the circle of racial life and interests. The Church furnishes the widest arena.
It is seriously to be questioned whether any
people in the present stage of the negro race
can be efficiently governed without the elements
of priestcraft. The negro, broadly speaking,
is hardly governed at all by the State, but
merely coerced and beaten into obedience. He
is not encouraged to have a sympathetic understanding of or a consenting part in the beneficent aims and objects of government. The
sheriff and the trial judge are the only officers
of the government with whom he is familiar,
and he meets with these only when his property
or his liberty is in jeopardy. If it were not
for the Church, the great masses of the negro
race would be wholly shut off from any organized influence touching them with sympathetic
intent. As imperfect as is the negro church in
many of its features, it is the most valuable
ally of the government. Eliminate the Church
and the task of governing this people on part
of the State would be more than doubled in
difficulty.

Within the Church the opportunity for the
talented tenth is almost unlimited. The negro
preacher has a larger influence and function
than his white confrère. He is not only the
spiritual adviser of his flock, but also their

guide, philosopher and friend. Almost every feature of leadership and authority comes within his prerogative.

Those who stand in the high places of moral and spiritual authority among the people ought to represent the highest intelligence, character and manly powers. In this arena the talented tenth may exploit its talent without let or hindrance. Here is the one unlimited field already white unto the harvest. Let none imagine that, because people are ignorant and lowly, their moral and spiritual leaders do not require all discipline, learning, culture and practical wisdom that the completest education can afford. The more ignorant the led, the more skilful and sagacious should the leader be. If the blind lead the blind, will not both fall into the ditch? To partake of the things of God and show them to this simple-souled folk requires the deepest insight into things scientific, social and spiritual. No one can be too learned or too profound to whose direction has been committed the temporal and eternal destiny of a human being.

THREE RELATIONS

The negro in his Church affiliations sustains three more or less distinct relations to the great ecclesiastical organizations with reference to control.

(1) In the Presbyterian, Congregational and Episcopal churches he sustains a dependent or missionary relationship. The parent organizations in large measure supply the means for supporting the churches and furnish general direction and control. The negro minister has complete charge over the immediate matters of his individual congregation, but in the larger matters of general plans and policies he has little or nothing to say. His numbers are so small that he is regarded as a negligible quantity in the general equation.

(2) The colored membership of the Methodist Episcopal Church constitute a sufficiently large element to impress considerable influence on the general life of the connection. They enjoy all but complete local independence in their quarterly and annual conferences. The white bishop does little more than register the decision of his colored cabinet, and serves as a guarantee that the procedure shall be in harmony with the connectional discipline. The colored churches are self-supporting and have a proportional voice in all of the deliberations of the General Conference. They are numerous enough to be reckoned with in all important plans and policies for the general life of the

Church. In the missionary and educational work the two races are brought into friendly and helpful relations. The negro element has the opportunity to study at first hand the intimate workings of one of the greatest organizations of the world.

(3) The great bulk of negro church members belong to those denominations which have cut loose wholly from all white control. These organizations are managed and manned from top to bottom by negro officials.

Each of these modes of relationship has its advantages and its disadvantages. But the logical and inevitable tendency is toward negro ecclesiastic autonomy, and must continue so, as long as the evil spirit of prejudice seeks and finds lodgment in the Christian Church.

ECCLESIASTICAL INDEPENDENCE

There are 30,000 negro religious organizations reporting over 3,600,000 communicants. The value of the property involved amounts to $56,000,000. This wonderful religious development is found mainly in the Baptist and Methodist denominations, which from the start assumed ecclesiastical independence. The Presbyterian, Congregational and Episcopal denominations, which have enjoyed the greatest measure of white contact and control, have thriven but feebly, at the expense of much watering, as a root out of dry ground. While there is a certain orderliness and decorum of procedure, the spirit and puissance which spring from the conscious power of self-propulsion are wanting.

They fail to arouse the people and inspire them with spiritual enterprise and aggression. The more thoughtful leaders of these denominations are beginning to appreciate the heavy handicap of their subordinate positions. Annual conferences are being held of the colored segments of these several bodies in which the sprouting spirit of ecclesiastic self-control is beginning to assert itself. There are nearly 200,000 negro members of the Methodist Episcopal Church who, up to the present time, have maintained loyal vassalic relations to the parent body. But the more ambitious and aggressive spirits among them are becoming restive, even under such a complaisant subordination, and are already formulating a declaration of ecclesiastical independence.

The negro church is the most effective expression of the desire for self-government. It has been abundantly demonstrated that the church life of the race will not thrive on any other basis.

Business Talent Required

The negro minister in the conduct of his church often transacts a greater volume of business than any other member of the race in his community. He should be a business man as well as a spiritual adviser. Because of the general business inexperience of his membership, it is necessary for him to understand business principles and methods in church management. The most striking indication of worldly success among negroes is not seen in the business places which they conduct, but in the magnificent churches which they control. Whatever claims may be made for the ministry on its sacred side, in its financial feature it is as much a business as any other material interest. By virtue of his confidential relation to his membership the minister often becomes their financial adviser. He inculcates the spirit of economy and thrift—advises the inexperienced men of his congregation to start bank accounts and directs them in the purchase of property. The ministry affords a splendid field for the educated negro to exercise business as well as spiritual talent.

This immense religious estate requires 20,000 ministers and managers to conduct its affairs. In the larger cities there are costly edifices ranging from $50,000 to $100,000 in value, with an annual fiscal budget of from $5,000 to $20,000.

THE BAPTISTS

Even in the smaller cities and towns, especially among the Baptists, it is easy to find churches counting from 500 to 2,000 members over whom the pastor exercises as complete and as effective control as many a king on his first-class throne. When we consider that a colonel in the army has under him only a thousand men, the influence and power of the negro Baptist preacher begins to loom upon us. According to the policy of the church, the local pastor is supreme in his jurisdiction, and the larger opportunities for connectional activities afforded by the more highly organized bodies are counterbalanced by the intensity of his local sway. Although his principality is small, there is no authority higher than that of the prince.

THE METHODISTS

The Methodist churches have a smaller membership, but a more perfect scheme of organ-

ization. There are twenty-six bishoprics in
these several bodies. A bishop controls more
persons and exercises greater authority than
a general in the army. These positions carry
with them more authority, dignity and power
than any other openings to which the negro
youth can reasonably aspire under our civilization. These 30,000 pulpits and twenty-six
bishoprics, together with numerous collateral
and connectional offices, must be filled in this
generation; and they ought to be filled by the
most highly endowed and gifted of the race.
Every man of them should be a worthy workman that maketh not ashamed.

The Unlettered Negro Minister

The vast estate has been built up by comparatively unlettered and untrained men. This
is indeed the one miracle of the age. Here was
a set of men without preparation or announce-
ment, like Melchizedek of old, stepping at one
bound from the cotton patch into the pulpit,
and from the barber's chair to the bishop's
bench,—from the humblest to the highest human pursuits; and, with all of their disabilities,
they have succeeded in organizing and holding
together so great a body in Christian fellowship. That there have been imperfections,

grossness and grotesqueness goes without saying. But the great, outstanding, concrete fact
remains that this religious estate has been developed and handed down to the rising generation as its most valuable inheritance.

When the Church history of the past fifty
years shall have been written these humble unlettered priests of God will be accorded a high
meed of praise which is their just due. All of
the money and effort that have been expended
for missionary purposes throughout the world
for the past two generations have not brought
as many souls into the folds of Christian
churches as these ignorant black preachers,
who are too often held up to ridicule by the
more haughty Christian co-workers who are
disposed to hide even as it were their very
faces from them.

RIGHTEOUSNESS OF DOCTRINE

I have listened to negro preachers of every
degree of ignorance and ungainliness. I have
heard them indulge in many utterances that
seemed to me to be crude, grotesque and absurd. But I have never in a single instance
heard the pronouncement of a doctrine that
did not point in the right direction. It is
doubtless true that in many instances the life

of the preacher did not square with his preachments. Even the Apostle Paul appreciates the
possibility that he might himself be a cast out
while being the means of saving many.

The ignorance of the negro ministry of the
generation just past and now passing is the
kind of ignorance that God Himself winks at;
but He will not wink at this ignorance if it is
allowed to continue in the generations to come.
Great indeed will be the condemnation of this
generation if it allows this sacred office to be
conducted by ignorant and incompetent men.
Their forbears, whose prayers, in the darker
days, went up to the throne of God from the
low grounds of sorrow, will rise up and condemn such spiritual degeneration. But, great
as will be the condemnation of this generation,
it will be excelled by its folly, if it neglect so
great an opportunity.

Let me repeat here what I said in another
place. ''The Church is not merely a religious
institution, but embraces all of the complex
functions of negro life. It furnishes the broadest field for the exercise of talent, and is the
only sphere in which initiative and executive
ability can abound. Frederick Douglass began
his public life as a local preacher in the A. M.
E. Church, and, if a wider career had not provi-
dentially opened up to him, he doubtless would

have risen to a position of ecclesiastical dignity and power. In politics, education and business the white man manages and controls the negro's interests; it is only in the Church that the field is undisputed. Upon the failure of the Reconstruction governments, the negro politicians sought careers in the Church as the most inviting field for the exercise of their powers. The negro preacher is a potential politician, whose natural qualities of organization and leadership, being denied scope and exercise in the domain of secular activity, lead him to seek them in the religious realm. When the negro preacher makes occasional excursions into the political field we are apt to condemn his conduct as irrelevant to his calling, but he is merely giving vent to pent-up powers on the slightest show of opportunity or pretext of duty.''

SPOKESMEN OF THE PEOPLE

The negro preacher will be the spokesman of the people because his support comes directly from them. The teacher, on the other hand, whose stipend is controlled by the officers of the state, dares indulge in only such utterances as will not displease those upon whose good graces his tenure of place depends. If the honest untrammeled voice of the race, stating its own case and pleading its own cause, is ever to be heard and heeded, it will come from or be supported by the negro pulpit. There can never be stable equilibrium until the center of gravity falls within the basis of support. He will be the daysman and peacemaker between the races. The uplift of the race is largely in the hands of the clergy. If the pulpits and bishoprics and other high ecclesiastical stations could be filled by the men of the best intelligence, character and consecration within the race, all of its complex problems would be in a fair way toward solution. It is a sad day in the life of any people when ''the best they breed'' do not seek the highest and holiest of all callings; but sadder still will it be for a retarded people if its ministry remains in the hands of those illy prepared to exercise its high functions.

Pulpit Uplifts the People

The uplift of negro ministry means the uplift of negro life; the downpull of this ministry means the pulling down of the people. The most effective way to improve the general moral, industrial and social tone of the race is to elevate its pulpit. Outside philanthropy cannot be indifferent in the proposition if it

purposes to aid the race efficiently. Philanthropy can only furnish the first aid. It en-
courages the leaders; they must do the rest.
The only help that is helpful in the long run is
that help which helps the helped to help themselves.

SLIGHTING THE MINISTRY

Educated negroes are not entering the ministry in such numbers as might be expected
when we consider the opportunities afforded by
this high calling. There is, on the other hand,
a tendency away from the ministry on the part
of the negro youth with splendid educational
equipment. During the past twenty-five years
the colored public schools of Washington, D.
C., have not furnished a half a dozen candidates for the ministry out of the several thou-
sands who have completed the High School
courses within that time. I do not now recall
a negro graduate from a Northern college
within the past ten years who has entered upon
the sacred office. A very small proportion of
the graduates of the negro colleges are turning
in that direction. The educated men have not
yet in considerable numbers turned their attention to the larger opportunities of the Baptist and Methodist churches. This indifference
or neglect is due to the natural feeling which

the educated man has against too close affiliation with the more ignorant body of clergy now filling these stations. It is also in part due to the prevailing tendency of the times, which seems to be away from the Church. The white race is complaining that it is almost impossible to induce the ablest young men to enter the theological seminaries preparatory to the sacred office.

Attractive Secular Pursuits

Among the whites, however, there are various other lines of opportunity which prove equally or even more enticing to the aspirations of ambitious youth. Politics, business, law, medicine, journalism, literary and leisurely pursuits conspire to rob the ministry of its former claim as an exclusive field for the high powers and talents. In the earlier years the graduates of Harvard, Yale, and Princeton mainly were recruited to the ranks of the ministry, not so much because they were more pious and consecrated than they are now as because the ministry at that time afforded the one great field for educated men. The negro race to-day is in the same relative position which the white race occupied a hundred or more years ago. The ministry requires and can maintain a larger number of educated youth than all of the other so-called learned professions combined.

When the talented tenth awakens to a realizing sense of the demands and opportunities of the situation then will the tide turn toward the ministry as to a harvest field ready for the reaper.

The Higher Aims of the Ministry

I have so far avoided dealing with the mystic side of religion or of the sacerdotal office. The negro has a high religious and emotional endowment. Those who are endowed or endued with a double portion of this power will feel the "cosmic urge" impelling them to consecrate themselves to the work of moral and spiritual awakening. Without a conscious sense of this enduement, the pursuit of the ministry as mere enterprise is unworthy the contemplation of an honest mind.

It has been my purpose to point out in concrete terms the opportunities which the ministry affords the talented tenth, which will, of course, be doubly enhanced by the higher claims of the sacred office, which always render the devoted priest "more skilled to raise the wretched than to rise."

THE ULTIMATE RACE PROBLEM

The adjustment of the forward and backward races of mankind is, without doubt, the most urgent problem that presses upon the twentieth century for solution. The range of this problem is not limited to any country or continent or hemisphere; its area is as wide as the inhabitable globe. The factors involved are as intricate in their relations, and as far-reaching in their consequences, as any that have ever taxed human wisdom for solution. A problem as wide as human interest, and as deep as human passion, will not yield to hasty nostrums or passionate dogma, but calls for statesmanlike breadth of view, philanthropic tolerance of spirit, and exact social knowledge.

The local phase of this question in the United States has become so aggravated and acute that our solicitous philosophers are prone to treat it as an isolated phenomenon, separate and apart from the worldwide problem of which it forms a fragment. But the slow processes of social forces pay little heed to our fitful solicitude. Indeed, the bane of sociological endeavor is the feverish eagerness of the extemporaneous reformer to apply his premature program of relief to every local symptom, without adequate knowledge of social law and cause. We get a broader and better grasp on the race problem in America, when we view it in the light of the larger whole. As the astronomer cannot divine the course and career of a particular planet without a broad knowledge of the underlying laws that govern the solar system, nor the naturalist gain any adequate notion of a single animal or plant unless his observation and study are based upon a general conception of the species to which it belongs, so the student of social problems will not wisely draw conclusions from a single contributory factor, to the neglect of the general product. In the great social scheme of things, the adjustment of man to man is a unitary problem, and the various modes of manifestation, growing out of place and condition, are but parts of "one stupendous whole."

In attempting the solution of any problem of a social nature, we should first seek to separate those factors that are universal and unchanging in their operation from those that are of a special and peculiar nature. The primary principle, which runs like a thread through all human history, is the communicability of the processes of civilization among the various branches of the human family. This is, indeed, the determining factor in the solution of the universal race problem that confronts the world to-day.

It so happens, in the process of human development, that the whiter races at present represent the forward and progressive section of the human family, while the darker varieties are relatively backward and belated. That the relative concrete superiority of the European is due to the advantage of historical environment rather than to innate ethnic endowment a careful study of the trend of social forces leaves little room to doubt. Temporary superiority of this or that breed of men is only a transient phase of human development. In the history of civilization the various races and nations rise and fall like the waves of the sea, each imparting an impulse to its successor, which pushes the process further and further forward.

Civilization is not an original process with any race or nation known to history, but the torch is passed from age to age, and gains in brilliancy as it goes. Those who for the time being stand at the apex of prestige and power are ever prone to indulge in "Such boasting as the Gentiles use," and claim everlasting superiority over the "lesser breeds." Nothing less can be expected of human vanity and pride. But history plays havoc with the vainglorious boasting of national and racial conceit. Where are the Babylonians, the Assyrians and the Egyptians, who once lorded it over the earth? In the historical recessional of races they are "one with Nineveh and Tyre." Expeditions must be sent from some distant continent to unearth the glorious monuments of their ancestors from beneath the very feet of their degenerate descendants. The lordly Greeks who ruled the world through the achievements of the mind, who gave the world Homer and Socrates and Phidias in the heyday of their glory, have so sunken in the scale of excellence that, to use the language of Macaulay, "their people have degenerated into timid slaves and their language into a barbarous jargon." On the other hand, the barbarians who, Aristotle tells us, could not count beyond ten fingers in his day subsequently produced Kant and Shakespeare and Newton. The Arab and the Moor for a season led the van of the world's civilization.

Because any particular race or class has not yet been caught up by the current of the world movement is no adequate reason to conclude that it must forever fall without the reach of its onward flow. If history teaches any clear lesson, it is that civilization is communicable to the tougher and hardier breeds of men, whose physical stamina can endure the awful stress of transmission. To damn a people to everlasting inferiority because of deficiency in historical distinction shows the same faultiness of logic as the assumption that what never has been never can be. The application of this test a thousand years ago would have placed under the ban of reproach all of the vigorous and virile nations of modern times.

In present-day discussion concerning the advanced and backward races of men much stress is laid on what is called the white man's civilization, as if this color possessed exclusive proprietorship in the process. We might as well speak of the white man's multiplication table. It is impossible to conceal the secret and method of civilization as a quack conceals the formula of his patent nostrum. The lighted candle is not placed under a bushel, but on a candlestick, and gives light unto all who come within range of its radiant influence. We reward with a patent right the originator of a new process, guaranteeing him the benefit of the first fruit of the creation of his genius; but its value to the inventor is always proportional to the diffusion of benefits among his fellow men. And so the race or nation that first contrives a process or introduces an idea may indeed enjoy its exclusive benefit for a season,

but it will inevitably be handed down to the
rest of the world, which is prepared to appropriate and apply its principles. When a
thought or a thing is once given to the world,
it can no more be claimed as the exclusive property of the person or people who first gave it
vogue than gold when it has once been put in
circulation can be claimed as the exclusive possession of the miner who first dug it from its
hiding place in the bowels of the earth. The
invention of letters has banished all mystery
from civilization. Nothing is there hidden that
shall not be revealed. There can be no lost
arts in the modern world. England to-day can
utilize no process of art or invention that is
not equally available to Japan. The most benighted people of the earth, when touched by
the world-current, become at once "the heirs
of all the ages, in the foremost files of time."

There is in every potential cult the pent-up
spirit to multiply and expand itself. The impulse to disseminate as widely as possible that
which stirs our own feelings or moves our own
imagination is a law of social, as well as of
individual, psychology. It becomes the gospel
of glad tidings which we are constrained to
proclaim to all the people. "Go ye into all the
world, and preach the gospel to every creature" is a vital mandate that applies to every

type of civilization as well as to the religion of
Jesus. While it is true that it is only in religious propagandism that the missionary motive is conscious and purposive, yet the principles of secular civilization are no less effectively imparted because the altruistic motive
may not be a conscious part of the policy of
those promoting them. The blessings of a
higher civilization have always been vouchsafed
to overridden peoples by their ambitious ex-
ploiters, and its secret and method proclaimed
to "every creature" within the expanding circle of its influence. The self-seeking aggressor
becomes the unconscious missionary of the language, laws, institutions, customs, manners and
method of the higher form of development
which he represents; the soldier in quest of
dominion brings system and discipline; the
merchant's greed for gain introduces the comforts, conveniences and refinements of the
higher life; the pedagog looking for a livelihood spreads a knowledge of literature and
the subtler influences that minister to the
higher needs of the mind.

The European races are now overrunning
the world in quest of new resources to exploit,
and are thus coming into close and intimate
contact with the various weaker breeds of men.
The commercial spirit is the ruling passion of

the dominant world to-day. The whole surface of the habitable globe is practically parceled out among the stronger nations within defined spheres of influence. It is easy to predict the continuance of this process until "every creature" has been touched by modern civilization. The wonderful growth of exact knowledge and its application to the forces of nature is rendering this contact easy and inevitable. Steam and electricity have annihilated distance and banished the terrors of the deep; preventive and remedial medicine has neutralized the baneful influence of climate, and checked the ravage of disease; the hardship of pioneer life is lessened by the easy transportation of material comforts, and the loneliness of isolation is relieved by the transmission of intelligence which is flashed around the world swifter than the wings of morning. We may naturally expect that less and less heed will be paid to the fixity of the bounds of habitation of the various races and nations that dwell upon the face of the earth. The outcome of this contact constitutes the race problem of the world. As water when unrestrained flows from a higher to a lower level till equilibrium is established, so we may expect this stream to flow down and out from the higher fount until the various races and tribes of men reach an equilibrium of civilization and culture.

The place of education in human development is a principle whose importance is just beginning to dawn upon the world. Knowledge is the great equalizing factor in modern civilization. At one time it was thought that divine favor made one man lord over another. It was but a short step from the divine right of the ruler to the divine right of the race. But we are gaining a clearer and clearer conviction that racial, like individual, superiority depends upon knowledge, discipline and efficiency, which may be imparted largely by education. A peo-, ple may gain or lose its place according as it holds aloof from or keeps in touch with the highest attained efficiency of the world. The powers and forces of nature are not enchanted by any sorcery of race, but yield their secret and mystery to the application of knowledge. Steam and electricity, wind and wave and sunlight, will work as willingly for a backward as for a forward race. The only advantage that the latter possesses is a predisposition to a better discipline and a higher social efficiency. It does not appear that it possesses a better grasp upon the recondite principles of knowledge. Education can be relied upon to discount if not to liquidate the disadvantage under which the backward races labor. Nor is it necessary for such races to repeat the slow steps and stages by which present greatness has been attained. He who comes at the eleventh hour is placed on equal terms with him who has borne the heat and burden of the day in the vineyard of civilization. It takes the child of the most favored race twenty-five years to absorb the civilization of the world. The child of the backward race can accomplish the same feat in the same space of time. Japan is teaching the world that she can appropriate and apply the agencies of civilization as readily, and wield them as effectively, as the most favored nations of Europe. What Japan has done can be repeated by China or India, or Africa, or by any hardy people with territorial and national integrity who will assimilate the principles of modern progress through education and helpful contact with those nations which are now in the forefront of things.

There are three distinct modes of race-contact: (1) where the European takes up permanent residence among the weaker race, as in Australia, South Africa, and Hawaii; (2) where the white man has no expectation of permanent residence, but aims merely at political and commercial domination, as in India, North and Central Africa, and the Polynesian Isles;

and (3) where the weaker race has been introduced into the land of the stronger for the sake of industrial exploitation, as in the United States, South America, and the West Indian archipelago. The several phases of the race problem growing out of these different modes of contact are too often overlooked in current discussion.

The conceivable lines of outcome of race-contact are: the enslavement of the weaker, or, what amounts to the same thing, its subordination into an inferior caste; the extermination of the weaker or of the stronger; amalgamation or absorption; and amicable adjustment and continuance of distinct ethnic types. All of these processes will doubtless contribute in part to the solution of this problem. The outcome will not be uniform and invariable, but will depend upon the nature and complexity of underlying conditions.

In the United States this problem presents many interesting and unique phases which cause the student of social subjects to bestow upon it a degree of attention beyond that accorded any other point of race-contact throughout the world. Its workings are watched with the keenest interest, and much reliance is placed upon its indications, because it presents the widest types of ethnic divergence in the closest intimacy of contact.

(1) In this terrible process of race-attrition, millions of the weaker races will be utterly destroyed. Whole tribes and groups and sub-races will perish from the face of the earth. Civilization is a savor of life unto life and of death unto death, and its beneficence is reserved only for those who are endowed with power to endure. The red and brown races have faded before the march of civilization as a flower before the chilling breath of autumn. The Australian has gone; the red Indian has been dispatched to his happy hunting ground in the sky; many of the scattered fragments of the isles of the sea have vanished away, while others are waiting gloomily in the valley of the shadow of death. These people have perished and are perishing, not so much by force and violence, as because they were not able to adjust themselves to the swift and sudden changes which an encroaching civilization imposed. In Hawaii they have faded under the mild and kindly dispensation of the missionary of the Cross, quite as inevitably as if swept away by shot and shell. Even the American Indian has not succumbed so much as the victim of violence as the prey of the easily communicable vices of civilization. The frontier

of civilization will always be infested with socal renegades and outcasts, who flee from the light to hide their evil deeds. They carry with them the seeds of degenerative evil which destroy both mind and body. These become the consorts of the weaker race among whom they sow the seeds of death.

It seems that, where the backward race is thinly scattered over a wide area or thickly settled upon a limited territory, the white race is inclined to take up permanent settlement, which in the end is apt to lead to the destruction of the feebler element. After the disappearance of the eliminable elements the fittest, or, at least the toughest, elements will survive. The yellow and black races, through sheer physical toughness, have demonstrated their ability to look the white man in the face and live. They not only decline to vanish before his onward march, but actually multiply and replenish the earth in face of his most strenuous exactions. In India, in South Africa, in America, and in the West Indian Islands these races are increasing at a rate that plainly forbids the prophecy of extermination. Wherever the European establishes his high standard of governmental efficiency, checks the ravages of disease, and puts an end to internal tribal strife, these races have increased their strength at an accelerated ratio. Three-quarters of a million slaves in the United States in 1790, under the rigors of a slave régime, had swollen to four and a half million in 1860. While fresh importations from Africa contributed somewhat to this remarkable expansion, yet it was due mainly to the reproductivity of the original stock. From 1860 to 1900, during a transitory interval as trying as any people ever passed through, this four and a half million had doubled itself without outside reënforcement. The white, the yellow and the black races will doubtless constitute the residuary factors in the world's ultimate race problem.

(2) In the nomadic state of society, where population was only slightly attached to the soil, and roamed at will, without fixity of abode or permanence of abiding place, the expulsion of the feebler element was not an unusual outcome of race-contact. But under modern conditions, where the whole surface of the earth is preëmpted, and population irremovably rooted in the soil, the hegira of a numerous race from one land to another is the most absurd of all possible solutions. This method has been suggested as a possible outcome of the negro problem in America, but the proposition has always been regarded as an idle speculation. No publicist, who has regard for the san-

ity of his social judgment, would entertain it for a moment as a serious, practicable policy.

The temporary shifting of small groups of native peoples from one locality to another has been, and doubtless will continue to be, a minor process in the scheme of race adjustment. The American Indian is confined to reservations of diminishing boundaries, the Australian will be pushed to the outer verge of the island continent, the moribund remnants here and there will flee to the hills to hide them from the wrath of the approaching pale-face. But this is merely the preliminary stage of extermination which is the evident doom of these flying fragments. Where the weaker race constitutes the numerical majority, and thrives in multiplying numbers, the European is apt to withdraw under the sheer force of racial momentum. The white race has been expelled from most of the West Indian Islands, because the black race proved too prolific in such a congenial habitat. In the United States the whites are gradually growing relatively fewer in the black belts, and the bedarkened regions are steadily growing in intensity. Wherever any one of the hardier races is thickly settled it is not likely to be interfered with by competing numbers of any other race. Where the stronger race sends out only a handful of representa-

tives to command the superior governmental
and commercial positions, ultimate expulsion of
the stronger is the only predictable result.

(3) Wherever the white man has touched the
weaker races he has never scrupled to mingle
his blood with theirs. The sons of the gods
are ever prone to look lustfully upon the
daughters of men. There arises a composite
progeny which enters as an important factor
into race-adjustment. In this regard it is
necessary to make a sharp distinction between
the Teutonic and Catholic races of Europe.
The Latin or Catholic nations give the mongrel
offspring the status of the father, while the
Teutonic or Protestant races relegate them to
the status of the mother race. In one case the
white race becomes mongrelized while the
feebler element remains comparatively pure;
whereas, in the other, the white race remains
pure while the lower race becomes mixed. In
Cuba, where the Latin dispensation prevails,
the mixed element is returned as white; but in
the United States it is classed with the negroes.
In Cuba, Porto Rico and South America the
mongrelization of the races is either an accomplished or an assured result.

The Mohammedan religion and the Catholic
branch of the Christian faith are, without dis-
pute, superior to the Protestant type in allay-

ing the rancor of race-passion. The amity of race feeling in Constantinople and Rio de Janeiro is in marked contrast with that at Richmond and Baltimore. If the Mohammedan and Catholic races were in the ascendency in the world's affairs, the mongrelization of races would assume a different aspect from what may be predicted under the dominance of the Teuton. But as these more tolerant races seem to have spent their forces as world-ruling factors, we may as well place the stress of attention upon what is likely to take place under the dominance of the more intolerant races of northern Europe. An increasing mixed breed will be the outcome of illicit intercourse between the white male and the darker female, and will be thrown back upon the status of the mother. Where the number of the weaker race is small in proportion, this will form an important factor in the final solution, but where the number is relatively large it may be regarded as a negligible quantity.

A continuous infusion of white blood would bring about a closer and closer approachment between the two types, until all social restrictions would be removed upon the disappearance of the ethnic difference upon which it rests. If the negro element in our American cities was not constantly reënforced by black

invasion from the rural districts it would be
easy to predict its final disappearance through
extinction and amalgamation. But in South
Africa, portions of the West Indies, and the
heavy negro states of America, race fusion
will have but little determining effect upon the
general equation.

According to the United States census of
1890, there were 956,689 mulattoes, 105,135
quadroons, and 69,936 octoroons. The proportion of negro blood in this admixture would
represent about 500,000 negroes of pure
blooded type. It must also be remembered that
illicit intercourse between the races is largely
limited to the mixed element, and there is likely
to be very little fresh absorption of undiluted
blacks. On the other hand the degree and
grades of admixture returnable in the census
represent but a small proportion of persons
actually affected by admixture of blood. It is
estimated that fully three-fourths of the colored race are affected by some slight strain of
white blood. The octoroon and the quadroon
class will be apt to pass over clandestinely to
the white race, in order to escape the inferior
status of their mother blood. Such transition
tends to widen the breach between the races.
The white race will take in only such homeo-
pathic dashes of negro blood as to remain sub-

stantially pure. The white blood already infused in the negro race will be more equably diffused and the colored American will represent a more solid ethnic entity, being brown rather than black in color.

We are forbidden to prophesy any general fusion of races by the sure knowledge that, when the white race becomes conscious of what it deems the evil of miscegenation, it bars the process both by law and public sentiment. In all the heavy negro states the laws forbid intermarriage between the races, and, even where there is no law, public sentiment is pronounced and unmistakable.

(4) There will be an attempt to relegate the backward race to an inferior status wherever the white race takes up permanent residence. When slavery was an accepted system throughout the civilized world, the process was simple and easy. But, in the absence of the fixed status of servitude, the same result is sought to be accomplished through connivance and cunning. This policy is most clearly noticeable in the United States. Although the negro enjoys theoretically all the rights and prerogatives of an American citizen, yet in public sentiment and in actual practice he is fixed to an inferior social, civil, political, and industrial

status. But this scheme of subordination can only be local and temporary.

A caste system must be like a pyramid, each layer representing a broader area than the one resting upon it. It is impossible to form a lasting system of caste with a superincumbence of ten white men upon the substratum of one negro. If the negroes were everywhere relatively as numerous as they are in some parts of the Southern states, and if the whites were not smothered out by numerical predominance, the permanence of caste might be counted on as a calculable factor. The slave system in America was doomed to destruction because the slave element was not sufficiently numerous to support the entire white population. Even in the South there were only five hundred thousand slaveholders, who controlled four million slaves, leaving six million free whites practically on the level with negro bondmen, a condition which could exist only until the non-slaveholding class became conscious of their condition. The free laborer of the North was the first to awake to consciousness of the fact that he was made the competitor of slave labor, a condition which he resented and resisted to the bitter end. The overthrow of slavery was due to economic as well as to moral and philanthropic causes. It is impossible to relegate the negro to any status without at the same time affecting a sufficient number of white men to make up the full quota of that status. Any degradation placed upon the negro laborer must react upon the white workman of the same grade.

The caste system in America is bound to fail, not so much from humanitarian considerations as because it lacks a sufficient physical basis upon which to rest. Abraham Lincoln possessed an illumined understanding. His motto that a country cannot exist half slave and half free is just beginning to be appreciated by those who are devoted to the study of our complex national problems. New England does not make a fixed status for the negro, because, as President Eliot informs us, she does not deem it worth while. The country at large will ultimately be brought to the view that it is not worth while to establish a separate and distinct status for a diminishing fraction of the total population.

(5) After the red and brown races shall have perished from the face of the earth; after the fragmentary peoples have been exterminated, expelled or absorbed; after the diffusion of knowledge has established a world equilibrium, there will be left the white, the yellow and the black as the residuary races, each prac-

tically distinct in its ethnic identity, and occupying its own habitat. We can only prophesy peace, amity and good will among these types, who will more fully appreciate than we do now that God has made of one blood all nations to dwell upon the face of the earth, within assignable bounds of habitation. Whether this will be but a stage in the ultimate blending of all races in a common world type transcends all of our present calculable data, and must be left to the play of the imagination.

I SEE AND AM SATISFIED

The vision of a scion of a despised and rejected race, the span of whose life is measured by the years of its Golden Jubilee, and whose fancy, like the vine that girdles the tree-trunk, runneth both forward and back.

I see the African savage as he drinks his palmy wine, and basks in the sunshine of his native bliss, and is happy.

I see the man-catcher, impelled by thirst of gold, as he entraps his simple-souled victim in the snares of bondage and death, by use of force or guile.

I see the ocean basin whitened with his bones, and the ocean current running red with his blood, amidst the hellish horrors of the middle passage.

I see him laboring for two centuries and a half in unrequited toil, making the hillsides of our southland to glow with the snow-white fleece of cotton, and the valleys to glisten with the golden sheaves of grain.

I see him silently enduring cruelty and torture indescribable, with flesh flinching beneath the sizz of angry whip or quivering under the gnaw of the sharp-toothed bloodhound.

I see a chivalric civilization instinct with dignity, comity and grace rising upon pillars supported by his strength and brawny arm.

I see the swarthy matron lavishing her soul in altruistic devotion upon the offspring of her alabaster mistress.

I see the haughty sons of a haughty race pouring out
their lustful passion upon black womanhood, filling
our land with a bronzed and tawny brood.

I see also the patriarchal solicitude of the kindly hearted
owners of men, in whose breast not even iniquitous
system could sour the milk of human kindness.

I hear the groans, the sorrows, the sighings, the soul
striving of these benighted creatures of God, rising
up from the low grounds of sorrow and reaching the
ear of Him Who regardeth man of the lowliest estate.

I strain my ear to supernal sound, and I hear in the secret
chambers of the Almighty the order to the Captain
of Host to break his bond and set him free.

I see Abraham Lincoln, himself a man of sorrows and
acquainted with grief, arise to execute the high decree.

I see two hundred thousand black boys in blue baring
their breasts to the bayonets of the enemy, that their
race might have some slight part in its own deliver-
ance.

I see the great Proclamation delivered in the year of my
birth of which I became the first fruit and beneficiary.

I see the assassin striking down the great Emancipator;
and the house of mirth is transformed into the Gol-
gotha of the nation.

I watch the Congress as it adds to the Constitution new
words, which make the document a charter of liberty
indeed.

I see the new-made citizen running to and fro in the first
fruit of his new-found freedom.

I see him rioting in the flush of privilege which the nation
had vouchsafed, but destined, alas, not long to last.

I see him thrust down from the high seat of political

power, by fraud and force, while the nation looks on in sinister silence and acquiescent guilt.

I see the tide of public feeling run cold and chilly, as the vial of racial wrath is wreaked upon his bowed and defenceless head.

I see his body writhing in the agony of death as his groans issue from the crackling flames, while the funeral pyre lights the midnight sky with its dismal glare. My heart sinks with heaviness within me.

I see that the path of progress has never taken a straight line, but has always been a zigzag course amid the conflicting forces of right and wrong, truth and error, justice and injustice, cruelty and mercy.

I see that the great generous American Heart, despite the temporary flutter, will finally beat true to the higher human impulse, and my soul abounds with reassurance and hope.

I see his marvelous advance in the rapid acquisition of knowledge and acquirement of things material, and attainment in the higher pursuits of life, with his face fixed upon that light which shineth brighter and brighter unto the perfect day.

I see him who was once deemed stricken, smitten of God and afflicted, now entering with universal welcome into the patrimony of mankind, and I look calmly upon the centuries of blood and tears and travail of soul, and am satisfied.